Taking [A]part

Design Thinking, Design Theory
Ken Friedman and Erik Stolterman, editors

Taking [A]part

The Politics and Aesthetics of Participation
in Experience-Centered Design

John McCarthy and Peter Wright

The MIT Press
Cambridge, Massachusetts
London, England

This book was set in Stone by the MIT Press.

Library of Congress Cataloging-in-Publication Data

McCarthy, John (John C.)
Taking [a]part : the politics and aesthetics of participation in experience-centered design / John McCarthy and Peter Wright.
  pages cm. — (Design thinking, design theory)
Title appears as: Taking [a]part.
Includes bibliographical references and index.
ISBN 978-0-262-02855-4 (hardcover : alk. paper)
ISBN 978-0-262-55259-2 (paperback)
1. Teams in the workplace. 2. Interpersonal relations. 3. Product design. 4. Project management. I. Wright, Peter (Peter Charles). II. Title. III. Title: Taking apart.
HD66.M38174   2045
658.4'022—dc23
2014017231

To Mary, Janet, Megan, and Maddy

Contents

Series Foreword

As professions go, design is relatively young. The practice of design predates professions. In fact, the practice of design—making things to serve a useful goal, making tools—predates the human race. Making tools is one of the attributes that made us human in the first place.

Design, in the most generic sense of the word, began more than 2.5 million years ago when *Homo habilis* manufactured the first tools. Human beings were designing well before we began to walk upright. Four hundred thousand years ago, we began to manufacture spears. By forty thousand years ago, we had moved up to specialized tools.

Urban design and architecture came along ten thousand years ago in Mesopotamia. Interior architecture and furniture design probably emerged with them. It was another five thousand years before graphic design and typography got their start in Sumeria with the development of cuneiform. After that, things picked up speed.

All goods and services are designed. The urge to design—to consider a situation, imagine a better situation, and act to create that improved situation—goes back to our prehuman ancestors. Making tools helped us to become what we are, and design helped to make us human.

Today, the word *design* means many things. The common factor linking them is service, and designers are engaged in a service profession in which the results of their work meet human needs.

Design is first of all a process. The word *design* entered the English language in the 1500s as a verb, with the first written citation of the verb dated to the year 1548. *Merriam-Webster's Collegiate Dictionary* defines the verb *design* as "to conceive and plan out in the mind; to have as a specific purpose; to devise for a specific function or end." Related to the word *design* is *draw,* with an emphasis on the nature of the drawing as a plan or map, as well as "to draw plans for; to create, fashion, execute or construct according to plan."

Half a century later, the word *design* began to be used as a noun, with the first cited use of the noun *design* occurring in 1588. *Merriam-Webster's* defines the noun as "a particular purpose held in view by an individual or group; deliberate, purposive planning; a mental project or scheme in which means to an end are laid down." Here, too, purpose and planning toward desired outcomes are central. Among these are "a preliminary sketch or outline showing the main features of something to be executed; an underlying scheme that governs functioning, developing or unfolding; a plan or protocol for carrying out or accomplishing something; the arrangement of elements or details in a product or work of art." Today, we design large, complex processes, systems, and services, and we design organizations and structures to produce them. Design has changed considerably since our remote ancestors made the first stone tools.

At a highly abstract level, Herbert Simon's definition of *design* covers nearly all imaginable instances of design. To design, Simon writes, is to "[devise] courses of action aimed at changing existing situations into preferred ones." (Simon, *The Sciences of the Artificial*, 2nd ed. [Cambridge, MA: MIT Press, 1982], p. 129). Design, properly defined, is the entire process across the full range of domains required for any given outcome.

But the design process is always more than a general, abstract way of working. Design takes concrete form in the work of the service professions that meet human needs. This broad range of making and planning disciplines includes industrial design, graphic design, textile design, furniture design, information design, process design, product design, interaction design, transportation design, educational design, systems design, urban design, design leadership, and design management, as well as architecture, engineering, information technology, and computer science.

These fields focus on different subjects and objects. They have distinct traditions, methods, and vocabularies that are used and put into practice by distinct and often dissimilar professional groups. Although the traditions dividing these groups are distinct, common boundaries sometimes form a border. When this happens, they serve as meeting points where common concerns build bridges.

Today, ten challenges that unite the design professions form such a set of common concerns. Three performance challenges, four substantive challenges, and three contextual challenges bind the design disciplines and professions together as a common field. The performance challenges arise because all design professions

1. act on the physical world;

2. address human needs; and

3. generate the built environment.

In the past, these common attributes were not sufficient to transcend the boundaries of tradition. Today, objective changes in the larger world give rise to four substantive challenges that are driving convergence in design practice and research. These substantive challenges are

1. increasingly ambiguous boundaries among artifacts, structure, and processes;

2. increasingly large-scale social, economic, and industrial frames;

3. an increasingly complex environment of needs, requirements, and constraints; and

4. an information content that often exceeds the value of physical substance.

These challenges require new frameworks of theory and research to address contemporary problem areas while solving specific cases and problems. In professional design practice, we often find that solving design problems requires interdisciplinary teams with a transdisciplinary focus. Fifty years ago, a sole practitioner and an assistant or two might have solved most design problems; today, we need groups of people with skills across several disciplines and additional skills that enable professionals to work with, listen to, and learn from each other as they solve problems.

Three contextual challenges define the nature of many design problems today. Although many design problems function at a simpler level, these issues affect many of the major design problems that challenge us, and these challenges also affect simple design problems linked to complex social, mechanical, or technical systems. These issues are

1. a complex environment in which many projects or products cross the boundaries of several organizations, stakeholder, producer, and user groups;

2. projects or products that must meet the expectations of many organizations, stakeholders, producers, and users; and

3. demands at every level of production, distribution, reception, and control.

These ten challenges require a qualitatively different approach to professional design practice than was the case in earlier times. Past environments were simpler. They made simpler demands. Individual experience and personal development were sufficient for depth and substance in professional practice. Although experience and development are still necessary, they are no longer sufficient. Most of today's design challenges require analytic and synthetic planning skills that cannot be developed through practice alone.

Professional design practice today involves advanced knowledge. This knowledge is not solely a higher level of professional practice. It is also a qualitatively different form of professional practice that emerges in response to the demands of the information society and the knowledge economy to which it gives rise.

In a recent essay ("Why Design Education Must Change," *Core77*, November 26, 2010), Donald Norman challenges the premises and practices of the design profession. In the past, designers operated on the belief that talent and a willingness to jump into problems with both feet gives them an edge in solving problems. Norman writes:

In the early days of industrial design, the work was primarily focused upon physical products. Today, however, designers work on organizational structure and social problems, on interaction, service, and experience design. Many problems involve complex social and political issues. As a result, designers have become applied behavioral scientists, but they are woefully undereducated for the task. Designers often fail to understand the complexity of the issues and the depth of knowledge already known. They claim that fresh eyes can produce novel solutions, but then they wonder why these solutions are seldom implemented, or if implemented, why they fail. Fresh eyes can indeed produce insightful results, but the eyes must also be educated and knowledgeable. Designers often lack the requisite understanding. Design schools do not train students about these complex issues, about the interlocking complexities of human and social behavior, about the behavioral sciences, technology, and business. There is little or no training in science, the scientific method, and experimental design.

This is not industrial design in the sense of designing products but industry-related design—design as thought and action for solving problems and imagining new futures. This new MIT Press series of books emphasizes strategic design to create value through innovative products and services, and it emphasizes design as service through rigorous creativity, critical inquiry, and an ethics of respectful design. This rests on a sense of understanding, empathy, and appreciation for people, for nature, and for the world we shape through design. Our goal as editors is to develop a series of vital conversations that help designers and researchers to serve business, industry, and the public sector for positive social and economic outcomes.

We will present books that bring a new sense of inquiry to design, helping to shape a more reflective and stable design discipline that supports a stronger profession that is grounded in empirical research, generative concepts, and the solid theory that gives rise to what W. Edwards Deming describes as profound knowledge (Deming, *The New Economics for Industry, Government, Education*, MIT, Center for Advanced Engineering Study, 1993). Deming was a physicist, an engineer, and a designer, and for him, profound knowledge comprised systems thinking and the understanding of processes embedded in systems, an understanding of variation and the tools we need to understand variation, a theory of knowledge, and a foundation in human psychology. This is the beginning of "deep design"—the union of deep practice with robust intellectual inquiry.

A series on design thinking and theory faces the same challenges that designers face as a profession. On one level, design is a general human process that we use to understand and shape our world. Nevertheless, we cannot address this process or the world in its general, abstract form. Rather, we meet the challenges of design in specific challenges in which we address problems or ideas in a situated context. The challenges that designers face today are as diverse as the problems clients bring to us. We are involved in design for economic anchors, economic continuity, and economic growth. We design for urban needs and rural needs, for social development and creative communities. We are involved with environmental sustainability and economic policy, agriculture competitive crafts for export, competitive products and brands for microenterprises, developing new products for bottom-of-pyramid markets and redeveloping old products for mature or wealthy markets. Within the framework of design, we are also challenged to design for extreme situations; for biotech, nanotech, and new materials; for social business; for conceptual challenges for worlds that do not yet exist (such as the world beyond the Kurzweil singularity); and for new visions of the world that does exist.

The Design Thinking, Design Theory series from the MIT Press will explore these issues—meeting them, examining them, and helping designers to address them—and more.

Join us on this journey.

Ken Friedman Erik Stolterman
Editors, Design Thinking, Design Theory Series

Preface

We began to write this book when the social and economic consequences of a systemic financial failure had generated for many people lots of noise with little clear communication, an awful sense of groundlessness, and a fragmentation of community and the public space. As a result of this failure, many people feel that the greed of others has cheated them of the life they imagined for themselves. They feel that governments and banks have fed them a line about the future they could imagine for themselves if they participated in a stakeholder society and that a division exists between dream sellers and everyone else when it all goes wrong. It is as if the system of exchange has been discovered to be based on illusions about participative democracy and culture. This systemic financial failure has already raised important questions about people's sense of agency and responsibility when they are drawn into events that they have no control over but that result in real consequences for them.

But we also began to write this book at a time when practice in many areas of design and research had become concerned with facilitating dialogue and participation. Community activists are challenging conventional discourses that explain social problems in ways they cannot identify with or work with, and they are developing alternative frameworks, ideas, and practices that empower them (Ginwright, Noguera, and Cammarota 2006). A similar commitment to participation can be seen in the campaigns of youth groups such as InnerCity Struggle and FIERCE! They stimulate participation in dialogue to disrupt ideologies that position inequality as natural and young people of color as without ability or as criminal (HoSang 2006).

Many artists and art collectives have also defined their art practices in terms of facilitating dialogue among diverse communities (Kester 2004; Bishop 2012). For example, Grant Kester describes the work of the Austrian arts collective WochenKlausur, in which conventional perceptions and systems of knowledge are challenged by bringing together people from opposite sides of a debate to create dialogue and social change. Kester argues that this kind of art project demands a shift in understanding of art and aesthetic experience as more performative and participative. But Claire Bishop warns that socially engaged participatory art walks a fine line between liberation and tyranny and challenges the politics and aesthetics of this movement. Such critical engagement with the politics and aesthetics of participation is essential if we are to realize the potential of this new participatory culture.

Through pervasive and ubiquitous digital technologies and the emergence of social media, crowdsourcing, citizen science, hacking, and do-it-yourself (DIY) digital making, the potential for a new participatory democracy is emerging in our everyday lives. This emergence represents a massive shift in our collective experience, and its potential to scaffold a citizen-led participatory culture represents an opportunity for those who research and design human-centered digital technology to shape a more egalitarian future. Human-computer interaction (HCI) and interaction design research have been slow to respond to this potential.

In its early years, HCI provided tools to augment people's cognitive skills. Now, HCI also is involved in creating media for communication, infrastructures, community interaction, and experiences for understanding ourselves and our lives. HCI accommodates a multitude of interests, activities, and concerns, and the developments we explore in this book are nowhere near its center. That is still occupied by tools and gadgets, even if research on them is now framed in terms of user experience (UX), a commercial imposter for the critical voices of experience that HCI could have at its center. Even though user experience as performative, participative, and discursive is still at the margins, it is involved and could become more involved by bringing relevant and challenging projects to the attention of a largely receptive audience.

The generative concept that pulls together these challenging projects and that characterizes the shift in practice and discourse for us is participation. In one form or another, participation plays a part in each of the boundary-pushing projects in our account of a minor but potentially significant shift in HCI. It marks them as different from many other HCI projects and often curiously similar to many dialogical projects in the arts. Perhaps owning them would require HCI to embrace more fully the aesthetics and politics of participation. As a starting point, we offer an account that leans on the work of socially engaged participatory artists and theorists and also on the political and social theories of Jacques Rancière and others. Rancière's critical analysis of emancipation and dissensus has the potential to link experience-centered and participatory design with the politics and aesthetics of participative experience.

We see the projects that are featured in this book as experiments in opening up creative spaces for participation. These projects are always open to the contingencies of situation and the participative experience of those who take part. They are precarious projects teetering on the edge of possibility and uncertainty. As we have worked on this book, we have been engaged with their openness and precariousness, sometimes unsure about where they were going but excited by the possibility in every encounter and concerned about where the dissensus within and between would take us. During the three years that it has taken to write this book, we have had an exciting and sometimes uncharted journey in dialogue with these projects, and we have learned from them how to move forward with the politics and aesthetics of participation in experience-centered design.

Acknowledgments

We would like to thank University College Cork and Newcastle University for supporting us while we completed this book.

Our deep thanks go all the members of the Digital Interaction Group at Culture Lab, Newcastle University. This is a special place. Many of the projects that we discuss in this book originate there, and everyone in the lab has contributed in one way or another to making the delivery of this book possible. Our special thanks go to Patrick Olivier, who always makes things possible; to Rachel Clarke, Jon Hook, Guy Schofield, John Shearer, Robyn Taylor, and Anja Thieme for such brilliant projects; to John Vines, whose ideas on configuring participation have helped us clarify our approach to participative experience in design; to Simon Bowen, John Bowers, and Rob Comber for their general support and critical thinking; and to Tess Denman-Cleaver for intelligent and sensitive proofreading.

Outside of Culture Lab, we would like to thank Bill Gaver and the team at Interaction Research Studio, Goldsmiths University of London; Mark Blythe at Northumbria University; Jayne Wallace and Nick Taylor at the University of Dundee; and Andy Dearden, Dan Wolstenholme, and the User-centered Healthcare Design team at Sheffield Hallam University for their collaborations on a number of projects and papers that have shaped the thinking in this book. Thanks to Kia Höök for invaluable feedback as an anonymous reviewer and, as always, Doug Sery has been a patient and supportive editor.

Many of the ideas developed in this book and some of the projects were supported by the RCUK Digital Economy Research Hub (EP/G066019/1) on which Peter is a co-investigator. Peter was also co-investigator on the RCUK *Landscapes of Cross Generational Engagement* Project RES-352-25-0030, which funded the Photostroller project at Jacob House. He was also co-investigator on the NIHR, CLAHRC- South Yorkshire, *User-Centred Healthcare Design*

Project, which supported BOSOP. Newcastle University kindly supported John McCarthy as visiting research fellow, allowing him to spend extended time with the Digital Interaction Group at Culture Lab getting to know the projects and the people.

And finally, our families have been very patient with us while waiting for this book to be finished, so thanks to Mary, Janet, Megan, and Maddy.

1 The Experience of Taking Part

Enchanting Encounters

In a space surrounded by a cityscape of skyscrapers, a fifteen-story tall plume of balloons sways in the evening sky. On the ground, a crowd of people holds onto handlebars with which the participants maneuver this massive structure, curving it in on themselves or pulling it in a straight line. They work in groups, each of which controls one of 140 modular, configurable carbon-fiber units that they had earlier assembled. Each of these units is supported by seven extra-large helium balloons, which contain sensors, LEDs, and microcontrollers. This is "Open Burble" (Haque 2010) and the form it takes is a combination of what the crowd wants and does and the impact of wind currents that vary with the height of the plume. The plume moves, twists, tangles, flutters, and suddenly ignites with color. As the people on the ground shake and pump the handles, their movements create color through the whole system. Their individual choices become an integral part of a spectacular experience that is many times their size and that they together have produced.

Sky Ear, another project from the same design group, is a glowing "cloud" of balloons and mobile phones, tethered to the ground with cables, released about one hundred meters into the sky. The nonrigid carbon-fiber cloud consists of one thousand extra-large helium balloons, each containing six ultra-bright LEDs that mix to make millions of colors. People on the ground call into the cloud flying above them and listen to the sounds of the sky. Their calls disturb the electromagnetic fields inside the cloud and alter the glow patterns of the part of the balloon cloud affected by their calls. Feedback within the sensor network creates ripples of light within the cloud.

The Open Burble and Sky Ear projects are examples of *participatory projects*. Although they are technically and conceptually different from each other—Open Burble is composed and assembled by those members of the public who control it during a performance and Sky Ear is designed and assembled in advance with the public's only involvement on the day being to dial in a phone number that connects them to a specific balloon—they are both designed to rely on public participation for their realization as enchanting and sometimes challenging public events. Although the former combines making and use into a participative experience, the latter limits the experience of participation to interaction during performance.

Our interest in participatory projects crystalized when we saw videos of Open Burble and Sky Ear, and heard Usman Haque talk about these and other projects at the CHI 2010 Conference in Atlanta, Georgia. We had been involved in participatory projects and talking about participative experiences for a while without having developed a way of framing them. Reflecting on Haque's presentations, we decided that our interest in participatory projects was in their use of digital technology to create opportunities for people to construct and share new participative experiences together, whether through design and making or in use, whether to create new fun experiences, or whether to transform lives. Following on from our earlier work (McCarthy and Wright 2004; Wright and McCarthy 2010), we wanted to inquire into how participants and researchers make sense of participative experience and what value they take from it. It seemed to us from our experience with participatory projects that there could be many answers to these questions, some of which would entail rethinking the meaning of traditional human-computer interaction (HCI) categories such as designer and user, maker and developer, researcher and participant (Wright 2011), and some of which would suggest various modes of participation, participative experience, and various relationships among them.

When we heard Haque present Open Burble and Sky Ear, he described them as "dynamic, responsive and conversant" architecture. The projects explore novel forms of interaction and subtle forms of participation among the general public, technology, and a cloud structure, using digital media. Each time it is launched, Open Burble becomes an open system, an opportunity for participative experience conjured up by an unfinalized form, and an invitation to take part in "a participant-focused constructional system" in which nothing exists until participants enter into conversation with the artifact. The conversational metaphor appropriately reflects the potential for each participant to produce output that surprises the others and that requires a meaningful response from them. As is the case with many participatory projects, Open Burble and Sky Ear also engage in conversations that reach beyond the challenges of the design and use of their technology. They engage in a dialogue about public space and how it is conceptualized and realized in people's lived experience of the city. By taking part together in events that speak, at least for the span of an event, to the architectural realization of space, participants see people coming to appreciate their agency in these potentially overwhelming contexts. They see potential for a digital architectural experience to create dynamic spaces that respond to them. As projects exploring participative experience, they draw attention to an epistemology of participation that is itself participative, affective, and discursive, and a methodology that depends on the close relationship between experience and agency.

The broad aim of this book is to open up a space for creative, critical enquiry into the potential of participatory projects to enrich our lived experience. Although we have mentioned only two participatory projects so far, some of their similarities and differences and some of the conditions for their realization are already apparent. The more participatory projects we look at, the clearer it becomes to us that, even though participatory projects differ from each other in ways that should be explored, there is value in seeing them as a coherent, responsive movement. To give some shape to the variety of projects we will discuss, we have identified four genres of participation: understanding the other, building relationships, belonging in community, and participating in publics.

The remainder of this chapter will set the scene for our enquiry by examining why it makes sense to suggest that participation is the concept that gives coherence to the projects we will consider and introducing some participatory projects to give a flavor of the variety before discussing them in detail in later chapters. We will then outline our particular experiential approach to understanding these projects and participative experience more generally.

Why Participation?

The concept of *participatory project* marks out a space that can be differentiated from other movements in HCI, such as cooperative design and participatory design (Simonsen and Robertson 2012; Carroll and Rossen 2007). Participatory projects explore and harness the capacity of people to create participative experiences. These projects design for skillful, resourceful, situated persons to enable them to take part in new ways of defining themselves and their relationships with others, for example, what it can mean for someone untrained in interaction design or music to take part in something that enables them to play with new ways of being for a while and to contribute to the making of something of value to others. In these projects the participative experience unfolds in situations that are carefully designed and constructed to be responsive to the decisions and actions of those who take part. As well as being technically and conceptually challenging, these projects are also precarious, designed to be open to the possibility of not happening at all or not happening in anything like the way originally planned.

The distinctiveness of the participatory cultures of Web 2.0 (Jenkins 2006, 2009) also lies in the initiatives that "ordinary people" take to make them happen and to keep them happening. Within such cultures participation is not a simple all-or-nothing phenomenon or even a single linear dimension from, for example, active to passive or from token to full participation (Arnstein 1969). Rather, there is a qualitative emergence of possibilities. For example, Simon (2010), writing about participation in museums, argues for distinctions between those who contribute video to sites such as YouTube; those who comment, critique, and vote (like or dislike); those who create channels; those who consume; and so on. All these forms of participation can be undertaken by one and the same person over time or even at the same time. Simple role-based distinctions such as *user* and *designer, producer* and *consumer,* which attempt to finalize who people are in terms of what they do, thus become problematic.

Moreover, within such participatory cultures there are low barriers to personal expression and public engagement, strong support for creating and sharing, and sometimes mentorship whereby more experienced members pass on their expertise to those less experienced. In participatory culture, members believe that their contributions matter and feel some degree of connection with each other. We have previously written about participatory social media sites such as DiabetesMine, which was initiated by Amy Tenderich, who was diagnosed with type 1 diabetes at the comparatively late age of thirty-seven and found little information or support to help her understand and deal with the disease (Wright and McCarthy 2010). According to Tenderich, participation in the transformative context of Health 2.0 technology has made the information sharing, mutual support, and political identification that constitutes the DiabetesMine community possible. When taken together with similar developments in areas such as living heritage and participatory museums (Simon 2010; Giaccardi 2012) and community activity (Verasawmy and Iversen 2012; Frohlich et al. 2009), this has led to the idea of Web 2.0 supporting a full-blown citizen-led participatory culture.

It would be a mistake to create a promise of unhindered potential and expressiveness about participation. Social and political processes, including participatory projects, can be used to control as well as to liberate. Participation sometimes initiates dialogue that suggests contrasting positions or incommensurabilities, rather than mutual support and understanding. For example, the StoryBank project (Frohlich et al. 2009), in addition to exciting a burst of creativity in the small village of Budikote in southern India, also resulted in disagreements between stakeholders about the values they associated with participation in rural development projects. In partnership with two nongovernmental organizations (NGOs) in Bangalore, VOICES and MYRADA, who provide media infrastructure and run the local radio station, respectively, the StoryBank project made digital storytelling and sharing accessible. Quite a large number of people from the village joined in the project, authoring and adding their own stories to a shared community repository. Uploading the stories and viewing them, often in groups of up to fifteen or twenty people, became important and enjoyable social opportunities to share stories with friends, family, coworkers, and other group members. Villagers enjoyed stories from all categories but enjoyed health, education, and entertainment stories most.

Conflicting views among partners about the use of technology for development, inclusion, democratizing participation, and bridging digital divides brought broader cultural and political questions to the fore in StoryBank. The staff of MYRADA, who saw development as the pressing need for this community and as their main priority, felt that the personal and cultural information was of little value to development. They argued for better training and tighter control of content production and quality. In contrast, VOICES staff thought that one of StoryBank's main achievements was more democratic program making by a wide section of the community. They saw the personal and cultural contents as acknowledgment of the multifaceted nature of village life. For them, information could be enjoyed for its own sake and it didn't have to be seen exclusively as a means to self-improvement.

A focus on participation in HCI requires increased attention to social and political experiences with technology, including issues of ownership, authorship, and voice. The invitation to take part, including its terms and its consequences, the way in which it is made and by whom, puts these complex and evolving issues in play. The fact that it is an invitation colors how the engagement and interaction emerges and evolves. The complexities of people's relationships, their sense of themselves within participatory projects, and the critical and sometimes tension-filled experiences that result are usefully expressed by Bishop's (2012) analysis of the desire to overturn traditional relationships among art object, artist, and audience in participatory art projects. She identifies the following as the hallmark of this particular shift toward participation in the arts:

the artist is conceived less as an individual producer of discrete objects than as a collaborator and producer of *situations*; the work of art as a finite, portable, commodifiable product is reconceived as an ongoing or long-term *project* with an unclear beginning and end; while the audience, previously conceived as a 'viewer' or 'beholder', is now repositioned as a co-producer or *participant*. (Bishop 2012, 2)

Bishop has reservations about aspects of the participatory trajectory in the arts. Although she supports the broad ambition of politically and socially engaged art, she worries about a benign unquestioning acceptance of anything participatory or collaborative as inevitably good because of its ethic and about the possibility of art losing its distinctive voice. It is important to consider whether a focus on participation might also lead HCI away from its core values.

The Tyranny of Participation

It is easy to fall into the trap of assuming participation is not only an unqualified good but also a simple matter of consensus formation. The contested judgments in StoryBank and their implications for the meaning of participation are echoed not only in the arts but also more generally in debates about development policy and practice. Development is a politically sensitive area in which stakeholder organizations have strong views on the practice and purpose of development projects that color the kind of participative experience they are inclined to encourage. Some NGOs take quite a didactic approach, whereas others see themselves as facilitators. Some would judge their performance in terms of the efficacy of an intervention or the effectiveness of a program in terms of a predefined outcome, whereas others prefer to be led by the ways in which their interventions are received by the local community. Although most would advocate for and practice participatory development, some are concerned that participation can become a rhetorical commitment that brings about no real change in people's power to affect the situations in which they live, or worse, simply a bureaucratic hurdle to be jumped when promoting development programs.

In a collection of papers called *Participation: The New Tyranny*, Cook and Kothari (2001) suggest that the commitment to participation in development projects has gone so far beyond question and criticism as to be a "tyranny." They describe conversations occurring around participatory development conferences as follows:

the conversations with practitioners and participants were often characterised by a mildly humorous cynicism, with which tales were told of participatory processes undertaken ritualistically, which had turned out to be manipulative, or which had in fact harmed those who were supposed to be empowered. (1)

Cook and Kothari note that the ostensible aim of participatory approaches to development is to encourage people who are affected by development interventions, and who generally have no say in these projects, to become involved in the development process. Supporting the involvement of local people's perspectives and priorities, as an alternative to outside-led development, seems inherently right and, when adopted, is justified on grounds of empowerment, democracy, and sustainability. Each of these grounds would be seen by many as ethical imperatives in any engagement between people especially when they start from different positions of power.

Cook and Kothari note that some critical reflections on practice draw attention to the danger of participation resulting in political cooption and requiring contributions from participants in the form of unpaid labor, cash, or kind, transferring some of the costs of the project to the beneficiaries. However, beyond these methodological or technocratic limitations of participation in development, they more emphatically draw attention to problems with the politics of the discourse of participation. For example, they refer to some case studies in which participation functions in a project as a "system of representations," whereas local practice and local knowledge, far from shaping planning decisions and outcomes, is often structured by them (Mosse 2001). In these cases, participatory ideals are often constrained in practice by institutional contexts that require bureaucratic goals to be met. In another chapter, Cleaver (2001) shows how development bureaucracies' preferences for institutional arrangements that may not correspond to those of participants led to questionable assumptions about community and individual agency. The institutional rationale often posits simplistic assumptions about the rationality of participating, or not, that pay insufficient attention to the impact of changing and multiple identities on choices about whether and how to participate and that overlook links between inclusion and subordination. Clearly MYRADA and VOICES made quite different assumptions about the rationality of participating and the identities of participants in the StoryBank project. Viewed from one perspective, the participation of the villagers could be seen as a kind of innovative appropriation of the technology to subvert goals, taking the project off in new but interesting research directions. Viewed from another perspective it can be seen as a failure to tame the imaginations of villagers in service of their own developmental interests. At the heart of this

difference in perspective are two different understandings of the subjectivity of the villagers as participants.

The subjectivity of participants and researchers, and the experience they
have in participatory projects, is a central concern of this book. As we have
already seen, experience and subjectivity can be influenced by the qualities
of the activities that people are involved in, what is expected of them by
others and by social norms, and how they see themselves as participants.

Experience, Dialogue, and Participant Subjectivity

Participant is a slippery word. It is often used in research projects to refer
to those people (for example, members of the public) who volunteer or
are coopted as nonacademic, *lay* researchers (as opposed to professional
researchers), or as end users (as opposed to programmers or developers),
or as domain experts (as opposed to design experts). This complex web
of differences is centered on the subjectivities of professional researchers-
designers who configure public participants as the other. The question is
what kind of other? Suchman (2007) sharply highlights this point when
she describes how development teams can "configure" users as unruly and
likely to disturb their carefully controlled processes (Wright 2011). This is
something like the other as construed by the MYRADA staff.

In many projects the designers and researchers position themselves as
the subjective center of the project. From this position it is easy to configure the user as the unruly other, a stranger and an outsider who needs
to be tamed and trained. But it is equally possible to place the user (lay
researcher, domain expert, etc.) at the subjective center of a project and
enquire into how designers and researchers are configured as the unruly
others seeking to pry into in people's lives and impose certain kinds of
solutions rather than attending to real concerns. Either way, such precon-
figurations into hierarchical distinctions do not help in understanding participative experience.

Participants are positioned and position themselves in a variety of ways in
different projects, at different times, in different situations and relationships.
Participant subjectivity—by which we mean participants' sense of themselves as living, feeling, thinking people taking part in a project—is produced
by the discourses and the practices of the project, the things that they do as
part of these projects. Such discourses make available positions for people to
take up, ways of positioning themselves in relation to other people. So, for
example, Open Burble participants have a variety of positions made available
to them from which to explore creative subjectivities, a range that Sky Ear

does not make available, and, as we have just seen, two different NGOs in the StoryBank project have different preferences with respect to the positions that should be made available to the villagers who participate.

At the extremes, participants can be positioned as subjects or objects in a project, as creative people making things happen or as instruments for realizing the ambitions of others. The distinction between the two positions hinges on whether the participative experience is one in which voice and creativity are recognized in mutually responsive relationships. We refer to these to as dialogical relationships, relationships in which each party treats the other as differently placed centers of value, with different experience and expertise, people with feelings and values who can contribute to shaping their own and others' futures (McCarthy and Wright 2004; Wright and McCarthy 2010). When people treat each other in this way, each has the opportunity to see value in what the other has to say and to learn from listening to it. Over time, this can result in the kind of openness and mutual respect that fosters seeing the world from another's point of view and that, in some cases, results in the cocreation of new meanings, a defining feature of research enquiry in which researchers and participants learn from each other. When this happens, the experience of recognition can enrich participant subjectivity, enhance the prospects of mutually reinforcing relationships and a participative experience marked by feelings of creative engagement.

Participant subjectivity as it emerges and is sustained in relationships is the very point of some projects such as the Personhood project (Wallace et al. 2013; see also chapter 4). Working with Gillian, who at the time had mild dementia, and her husband and caregiver John, digital jeweler Jayne Wallace developed a cocreative process that involved the three of them getting to know each other very well over a long period of time and exploring together the experience of living with dementia, culminating in Jayne making digital jewelry pieces for them to share with their family. Because the experience of living with dementia is an encounter with the borders of personhood, the point of this project is participants' participatory subjectivities—that is to say, their sense of themselves and each other as living, feeling, thinking people. Jayne's approach invited Gillian and John to participate in a gentle, reciprocal enquiry. In conversations that recognized the distinctive roles of each of the three participants, space was created for all of them to exercise their particular creativity, individually and collectively. They worked together to understand the experience of living with dementia and to design artifacts to help support personhood in the experience. As we will see later, Gillian and John and the rest of their family played the major role in bringing meaning to the jewelry pieces that Jayne made for them. Participant subjectivity becomes a major focus of this project, the main concern of which is sustaining Gillian's personhood in her relationships with family and friends as her dementia develops.

The Personhood project, in contrast to Open Burble, shows us that participation can be quiet, intimate, private, and personal. Dialogue can occur in a gentle touch, a moment looking at a photograph, a reminiscence, as well as in shared stories about public walks and village events and the closely coordinated performance of flying Open Burble. Participatory design can be a slow journey taken by designers and participants as they define the design space and potential design interventions together or the construction of a digital infrastructure to facilitate a burst of creative community activity.

Participatory Projects as Dialogical Encounters

Open Burble, StoryBank, and the Personhood project differ from each other in a number of important ways, particularly in scale, technology, and context. In terms of scale, they range from multistory, responsive architecture and village media infrastructure to small family pieces that can be put in a pocket or a drawer. Technically, we have communication systems mediated by mobile phone infrastructure and lockets and music boxes mediated by local wireless networks. The contexts include the potential for collaboratively creating and experiencing enchanting public spaces, community creativity, and family conversations.

However these projects also demonstrate characteristics and commitments that help define their coherence as participative. First and foremost, they try to facilitate dialogue, the experiential and relational aspects of communication (Bakhtin 1984, 1986; Anderson, Baxter, and Cissna 2004). Open Burble requires participants to be present and responsive to each other and provides an infrastructure and a dynamic physical mode of interacting that promotes a deeply embodied interaction among participants. They feel and respond to each other's movements and in so doing participate in constructing an enchanting experience with each other. Haque's architecture is dynamic, conversant, and responsive on public and local intersubjective scales, with the overall dynamic swarm creating a challenging dialogue with the static architecture of the public square and the local interactive architecture facilitating dialogue among participants. The Personhood project invites a family to participate in the process of designing personal pieces that they all know will become a means of conversing with their wife and mother as she begins to lose some of her ability to remember. Their dialogue about family life and the anticipated experience of living with dementia is integral to the design process and, later, the appropriation of the jewelry. Because the engagement draws past experiences into the present to imagine the future, there is also a palpable dialogue between past and future in the lived present.

Although we use dialogic in general to refer to relationships among people, artifacts, texts, cultures, and so on, in this book we are specifically interested in dialogue between people (see Wright and McCarthy 2010). We use dialogue here to refer to something more than conversation or interaction. It refers to an open process of coming to an understanding that shapes and forms people even as they shape and form it. One's sense of self is formed in responsive communication with others, within which a growing recognition of the other person's perspective and voice as something other nourishes a growing sense of self with a distinctive voice and perspective. In this way the experience of dialogue creates rather than re-creates meanings, selves, and others. So when we say that participatory projects facilitate dialogue, we are suggesting that they support the constitutive processes through which these meanings, voices, and perspectives are experienced, recognized, and acted on. As different people perform and develop confidence in their own voices, diverging perspectives can come to the fore. So the participative experience is not likely to be harmonious at all times. In some cases, it can be at its most productive when the inherent tensions in dialogue are given air.

It is often in tension that the particularities of felt life are revealed. So, for example, instead of assuming the stability and continuity of a community, community is seen as forged in the relationships and interactions that encourage people to see signs of something called *community* in them, and those relationships and interactions are influenced by and influence the particular affective and political moments that constitute them. Moments of warm welcome, difference, and recognition, to name a few, characterize community for those living in it. Thinking dialogically about community involves sensitivity to those moments and to their institutional ramifications.

Acting in response to and in anticipation of the others' utterances involves taking part with them in a process that can transform how one understands oneself, others, and the world in which we live. *Transformative* seems to us to be an overused term in discourse on experience, relationships, and design and therefore at risk of losing its meaning and its power to affect and inform. And yet we do want to claim that participatory projects and participative experience can be transformative, can change the way in which we see ourselves and others as well as the way in which we act, even in small ways.

Transformative dialogical encounters involve engagement with other consciousnesses, other sets of values, other ways of thinking, in short, *otherness*. The differences between consciousness and counter-consciousness, one set of values and another, are the differences that specify a space between self and others even as they encounter and shape each other. It is in the struggle of bridging the space that transformation is made possible. Dialogical encounters are sometimes described as aesthetic experiences— imaginative and thoughtful, sensitive and sensual, emotionally fulfilling and valuable, transformative and distinctly felt by the people involved (McCarthy and Wright 2004).

Participatory Projects as Technological Imaginaries

As previously suggested, dialogues are creative engagements in which one's sense of self and sense of the world are formed in responsive engagement with others. We have already indicated that participatory projects can support dialogue by supporting the recognition of voices, perspectives, and meaning. The language of dialogical conceptualization can suggest local, face-to-face engagements among a small number of people, but this is just one kind of dialogical engagement. It provides a useful illustration of what we mean when we refer to dialogic, for example, its responsivity and openness, creativity and multivoicedness, even when those qualities refer to literary work, cultural tropes, and public debate. A dialogic novel is in communication with multiple other works, influenced by previous works and also influencing how they are read. Similarly public discourse on a topic, such as technology or community, can be responsive, open, creative, and multivoiced.

When we change our focus from local dialogical encounters to more public engagements, we see experiences and meanings of technologies, such as social media, formed as people respond to each other's interests and recommendations by taking part in particular uses of technology, and the subject of public discourse as strangers who share an interest in social media engage with each other in the process of becoming a public, a form of participation that we will discuss in chapter 6. Consider, for example, parents concerned about cyberbullying who engage in dialogue on social networks created for the purpose, or teenagers following each other in moving from a preferred social network site because their parents have become active on it, or people with diabetes joining DiabetesMine for information, social support, and shared advocacy. In each of these cases, we see experiences, meanings, and values of participatory technologies, and participation taking shape in imaginations and dialogues in the public sphere.

Shifting the focus from local encounters to technological imaginary highlights the role that publics, cultural milieu, and historical resonances play in the life and lived experience of technology. For example, although the invention of film is often associated with the work of Edison and the Lumière brothers, Punt (2000) demonstrates that the invention of film involved far more public participation than great inventor stories suggest. He used the notion of the technological imaginary to draw attention to the variety of ways in which people contributed to design of apparatus and negotiation of its meaning. The *technological imaginary* refers to "the ways in which technology was thought about both in terms of its hardware and as a representation of cultural aspirations—imagined and actual" (20). It also draws attention to the ways in which "the processes of imagining technology in the public sphere is significantly implicated in the processes of invention" (Punt 2000, 19).

A similarly interesting imaginary can be seen at work today in a number of participatory science projects. For example, citizen science projects bring together enthusiastic amateur scientists and appropriate networking and information-sharing technologies to collect and analyze data, develop technology, test phenomena, and disseminate results. Some crowdsourcing projects assign passive roles to members of the general public, using their computers to process data. In others, citizens collaborate with professional scientists to do science. Galaxy Zoo is a case in point. Here hundreds of thousands of participants classify millions of Hubble-generated images to identify galaxies. From quite early in the life of Galaxy Zoo, the citizen scientists formed complex self-organizing communities around specific interests or activities (Guardian 2012). Several Galaxy Zoo members are listed as coauthors on more than twenty scientific papers, a recognition of their active involvement in the making of science.

Some smaller-scale projects employ DIY making and hacking. Take DIYbio (Do It Yourself Biology), for example. Kuznetsov et al. (2012) describe it as a movement that aims to open source, tinker, and experiment with biology outside of professional settings. They see it as a grassroots movement and a platform open to everyone that builds on synthetic biology and identifies biology as a resource for tinkering or biohacking. Hence, it is not surprising that DIYbio has cultivated a close association with hacker cultures and practices.

DIYbio is an *imaginary*. The term refers to the way in which publics imagine their future world, not in theory but in stories, myths, and representations. In the case of technology, it not only refers to technology as they know it now and desire it to be in the future but also to what technology is not now but can or should be (Diocaretz 2006, 120): a dialogical version of technological imaginary, because participatory projects are less concerned with gadgets and devices and more with community and civic activity, less with commitment to finalization and closure and more with embracing openness and difference, less with individual invention and more with participatory practice, less with product and more with project.

It is arguable that in this ongoing dialogical imaginary involving people and ever-changing technology—past, present, and yet-to-be technology—that technology and values become a major focus of attention as the technologies' mediating interaction become transient. As this happens, the meaning of *user* in our participatory imaginary also has to be reconsidered. For example, the democratic entailment of a participative system evokes ideas of citizenship and personhood with respect to users. As our understanding of users and their relationship with designers evolves, and as the conditions and contexts of participation as "a mutual relation of influence and of evolution" (Diocaretz 2006, 118) is revealed, the detail of dialogical technological imaginary becomes pivotal in our reading of the projects that we will present throughout this book.

A Critical Enquiry into the Potential of Participation

Our enquiry is into a participatory technological imaginary, the myths that people are creating in participatory projects and publics, and the representations of participative experience entailed in the ways in which participation is embodied in the creativity of these projects and publics.

Our aim is to develop space for critical enquiry into the potential of participatory projects to enrich lived experience. Similar to most imaginaries, the participatory technological imaginary is still a work in progress as related practices, stories, myths, and representations continue to change and evolve. The participatory projects that we discuss are also generally in process, working out what participative experience and subjectivity mean in particular situations as the projects move toward provisional finalization. An enquiry into the potential of participatory projects is therefore an enquiry into participative experience *becoming* in the context of people's emerging sense of digital media. As an enquiry it is generative, its aim is not to describe what is already available, for example, a technological artifact, a social protocol, or a settled practice, but to engage with researchers and participants as they move toward something through which a dialogical participative experience could be realized.

The critical voice in this book is an appreciative voice, curious about the broader social value of the projects, interested in the experiences the projects support, and keen to understand what people like us, fairly mainstream HCI researchers and practitioners, can do with them. What can we learn from them to improve our projects and practices, most particularly what can we learn from them about involving people, users, and participants in our projects? And what can we bring to them as HCI researchers and practitioners? Our interest is in generating a dialogue around these projects that will provide the kind of insight into participation and participative experience that will yield a clearer understanding of what these projects are about, how we can all discuss their quality and qualities, and how the projects and practices that they embody can be evaluated, when evaluation itself may be a participatory attempt to understand their value in a variety of contexts and from a variety of perspectives.

It seems appropriate in a book about participation that our dialogical approach to enquiry aims for participation with the other rather than for professional privilege over them. There is a tendency in research to keep a professional distance from the subject of enquiry to be able to document and learn about it. This is generally an emotional distance that enables the researcher to produce an organized account by playing down the disorienting messiness of everyday experience. By contrast, participative enquiry treats content and experience as embodied in the lived experience and feelings of participants. As we have described in previous work, "content is never simply information to be retrieved or applied to particular situations but a sensuous and living engagement with a particular other" (Sullivan and McCarthy 2005, 634). Participating in dialogical enquiry with an other is a making process that involves learning to respond by "feeling the texture of their strangeness through creating it anew in the research process" (Sullivan and McCarthy 2005, 634). In producing this book this has entailed for us a kind of empathic engagement in which we try to move with the researchers and their participants as the project evolves and then to put that understanding into dialogue with our own process of writing. Tim Ingold (2013) puts forward a similar model of enquiry, arguing for a transformative focus in anthropological enquiry that would learn from and with others in order to explore human potential and being rather than learning about others in order to document what we know about the human condition.

In this book, then, critical enquiry means engaging with researchers and participants in their exploration into what participation and participative experiences might be like, grounded in responsive understanding of what it is like in particular projects, times, and places. Responsive in the sense that concepts and categories are not imposed on participative experience but rather the potential of each particular project as it develops is expressed in dialogue with participants and materials. The hope is that engaging with others in this way will bring about new ways of knowing and feeling, sharpening "perceptual, moral and intellectual faculties for the critical tasks that lie ahead" (Ingold 2013, 6). In practice, this has often meant taking part with project teams in exploring the participatory commitments and values that they display in their design processes and outcomes, and teasing out aspects of the relationships between designers and participants in their projects.

Understanding, working with, and evaluating the quality of event or participation is also made complex by the situated nature of quality in the context of these participatory projects. People will disagree with each other on the aesthetic and political merits of Open Burble, on their experience of participating in it, and on the relative importance of both. It is likely that people with different aesthetic and political positions, people who see public space and its commercial uses differently, will also disagree with each other on the very meaning of quality in this context and on what contributes to judgments of quality. We can see that quality—its meaning and its judgment—is likely to be a contested area even between these few projects. In related areas, for example the participatory arts, the very idea of judging quality is often frowned on.

However, it is difficult to imagine people not judging the quality of their experience, whether that experience relates to visiting an art gallery, playing a game, or doing a piece of work. In institutional contexts (particularly arts and humanities) there are often very good reasons to challenge the value of evaluation, including the diversity of ambition, the heterogeneity of project goals, the imbrication of ideological positions in work and judgments. Such objections are often not objections to evaluation per se but rather to a positivist approach to judgment and quality, which can have severe reductive implications theoretically and in terms of cultural policy and research policy. A focus on manifestly observable, readily measurable outcomes misses much of what participatory projects are about in a variety of domains. Such a focus can steer quality debate toward a limited set of disciplinary (e.g., high art or functional design) criteria or policy values (e.g., value added, impact factors, economic and social impact).

In the context of participatory projects, quality indicators ought to be contingent, responsive to the particular aims of specific projects and to the emergent participative experience that could be highly unpredictable. In terms of design and evaluation in participatory projects, a creative tension between different quality indicators—for example, some related to the artifact or system and others related to the participative experience—may be most productive. We can learn a little about what "productive" could mean in this context from other areas in which debate on the values of participation is already underway.

Bishop (2012), writing about value judgments in the participatory arts, argues that the meaning of quality in any particular setting is often contested and that the value judgments made in the name of quality are necessary "not as a means to reinforce elite culture and police the boundaries of art and non-art, but as a way to understand and clarify our shared values at a given historical moment" (8). Quality judgments of participatory projects in HCI could also be shaped to stimulate and inform debate about the values associated with participative experience. Such projects are also well aligned with the idea of quality judgments that reflect on the meaning and values of participatory projects and are sensitive to aspirations toward social engagement.

Scope of the Inquiry

It is not our aim to carry out a comprehensive survey of participatory projects in HCI. Given the nature of what we want to achieve and the need to know the projects we discuss very well, there is a bias in our selection toward projects in which we have had some involvement. As a result, we neglect many other projects that would have been equally valuable in illustrating the importance of participation. The projects we discuss are ones that have enchanted and intrigued us or that we know well through contact and collaboration. Many of them come from the Culture Lab in Newcastle, United Kingdom, with which we are both associated. We have been involved in these projects sufficiently to learn with and from them. Our hope is that most readers will appreciate that a deep understanding of the projects discussed is more important than comprehensive coverage.

Some projects are developed around a single staged event, some persist in time, and some can be seen to embody *eventness* as well as an extended temporal quality. For example, although Open Burble and Sky Ear are time-limited events, they are also moments in a longer-term project enquiring—through design of participative systems—into the subtleties of interaction, the politics of public space, and the experience of being a human in a digitally mediated environment. Some projects are tightly focused on local issues of participation in well-bounded events and others have a broader reach into issues of taking part in community or reflecting on one's public space. Because much of the energy of participatory projects as a movement in HCI is in this diversity and in how designers relate to the questions and challenges posed by such diversity, the framework that we will develop from chapters 3 to 6 addresses participation and participative experience through articulation of a number of different genres of participation. Although these genres differ from each other, the chapters describing them are presented as an unfolding of increasingly complex context in which participative experience develops.

Before we explore the genres of participation in chapters 3 to 6, we will first outline the qualities of the projects that we have brought together for the book. If participation and dialogue can span quite wide spaces, as we have suggested, what is it about them that we are asserting constitutes a movement, at least an inclination, in people's explorations of the potential of digital media? Many participatory projects involve more or less open systems that encourage subtle forms of participation by the general public without which the specific events or performances would never be realized. In these participant-focused constructional systems, the machines involved are treated as other onstage participants, taking part in collective performances that bring into play a variety of social relationships. In many projects, the focus is on the potential futures that these collective performances and social configurations suggest, which are explored in the design-centered enquiry that they provoke. In chapter 2 we describe a number of key themes or qualities that, taken in combination with each other, define the scope of participatory projects.

2 Themes and Genres of Participatory Projects

Themes

In this chapter we begin to develop our approach to understanding participative experience. We do this first by identifying and exploring four themes, which we see as characterizing the space of participatory projects we shall be concerned with. As we explore each theme we shall identify a number of qualities that are important. These qualities should not be understood as a set of requirements for membership but rather as an appreciation of the concerns that exercise participatory projects. The first is that participatory projects are best seen as design enquiries.

Participatory Projects as Design Enquiries

In using the term design enquiry rather than design research or research through design, we wish to create a space for a number of important moves in framing our participatory projects. The space we wish to sketch in this regard is one in which participants (including designers, researchers, and users) share a mutual curiosity and a commitment to explore and change something, learn together through the process, and achieve outcomes that may be collective and individual. The learning provides participants with new understandings and new opportunities for action and relationships. The outcomes may be different for the diverse individuals involved, a plurality of outcomes that creates important challenges for evaluation.

The commitment to enquiry, learning, and new perspectives means participatory projects are not the type of projects that participants approach as already committed to particular solutions or even to particular problems. Rather, participatory projects are characterized by open conversations and dialogue in which participants do not try to convince each other that their perspective is the correct one. Instead, they try to understand each other's perspectives and create ways of moving on, grounded in a mutual understanding of differences. A diversity of perspectives is thus central to these dialogues, because it is different subject positions borne of different experiences that enable new spaces of possibility to be opened up. To achieve this kind of openness, relationships of trust and empathy have to be developed between participants in order for them to feel safe enough to expose their own vulnerabilities and lack of knowledge and to share their experiences. A reflexive awareness of one's own effects on others in order to help them find their voice is essential to this process. But this open approach is not simply about letting everyone have a say. It is about a commitment to a view of design that believes transformative experiences come through the exploitation of difference to create a technological imaginary.

In an open, empathic, and critical questioning relationship, it is possible to construct new imaginaries through mutual learning. The point is not to create a team in which everyone becomes a designer. The dialogical perspective on empathy is not about fusing with another into a single entity; rather, it is about being able to understand how the other sees the world and to respond to that understanding from one's own subjective position. The commitment here then is to an ethics of participation, one in which equality is seen not as an endpoint achieved by colonization or assimilation of the other. Equality in diversity, in which each participant should be encouraged to have an equal but different voice in the process, is the starting assumption for participation. The plurality of experiences, perspectives, and expertise is the means by which the imaginary is achieved.

In many of the participatory projects that concern us, the focus is on the lived experience of those involved. But the aim is not to capture lived experience in order to abstract and reduce it to design requirements. Instead, the aim is to keep the experience alive in the design process so that it can be brought into dialogue with design expertise and ground the creation of a technological imaginary.

This aim of keeping experiences alive in the design process involves making them visible to others, and this requires trust. This is resonant with an approach to research in the social sciences called *participatory action research*. Participatory action research brings a participative worldview to understanding people and experience, and starts its enquiry from a view of the world as composed of "relationships which we co-author ... [in which] ... the 'reality' we experience is a co-creation" (Reason and Bradbury 2001, 6–7). This can be seen in clearest focus in Jayne Wallace's enquiry into personhood, sketched in chapter 1. In this project a close relationship of trust developed among Jayne, Gillian, and John, the couple living with Gillian's dementia, such that in her talk at the CHI 2013 conference she described them as "friends."

One of the tensions in practice for these designers and researchers is that, for professional and perhaps also personal reasons, most of them also want their local understanding to benefit their own academic and professional community of practice. This tension is apparent in most participatory projects and often plays out as a pressure to transform the kind of local knowledge and social imagination that is emergent from live encounters into a more distant reified disciplinary knowledge and insight. Researchers typically present their projects to their professional peers in forms that highlight their contribution to the discipline. The pressure to be concise, speak to issues that are alive in the discipline, and conform with genres of reporting that are typical of the discipline may work against ethical and aesthetic commitments to the voices of participants and to the aliveness of project experiences. Some courage may be required to call participants "friends" at a scientific conference but maybe that kind of courage is what is needed to ensure that the voices of participants are heard. Courage to challenge conventional forms of reporting notwithstanding, researchers who wish to do this will also have to give serious thought to the ethics and pragmatics of disclosure. Whereas including participants' voices in research reports may require a challenge to reporting conventions, the issue of keeping experience alive in design and in dissemination is conceptually and methodologically more difficult. Among other things, it requires sensibility and orientation to the ever-changing topography of participation and experience as it unfolds during a project.

Keeping experiences alive in design and in research is easily hindered by our habitual ways of thinking and making sense of the world. Raymond Williams (1977) suggests that we habitually convert lived experience into finished products by categorizing and theorizing. He argues that as we think about and make sense of experience, we place it firmly in the past, where it loses the living presence that makes it experience in the first place. Without that living presence, we cannot participate in it. This procedural mode of thought converts processes in which we are still actively involved into "finished products" or "fixed explicit forms" so that "living presence is always, by definition, receding" (128). It turns living indivisible wholes that are held together from within into assemblages of externally related parts. Following Ingold (2013), we would add that although we might learn a lot *about* a category—for example, architecture, dementia, family, caregivers—by studying the objects associated with it, we learn nothing *from* it. To learn from architecture, families, caregivers, or people with dementia, we have to enquire with them, not stand at an emotional distance from them, observing them.

In design and dissemination, the Personhood project worked hard against the tendency to turn the experience of living with dementia into finished products. Wallace brought her artistic sensibility and her empathic relationship with Gillian and John to bear on all discussions of how we would write about the project as a piece of research. The challenge was to conceptualize the project in a way that colleagues would find valuable and useful without draining it of the lived experience that Jayne had encountered and of the strong, personal relationships that constituted it. We approached this as a challenge to find a way of writing that had participative experience in it. Participants' voices—not just extracts from interviews but their concerns and perspectives—were aired extensively in accounts of the experience of dementia that emphasize the everyday and avoided the abstracted categorizations of outsiders such as clinicians and psychologists. Interestingly, this resulted in texts that proved difficult to publish in HCI, a field that is interested in everyday experience but perhaps still wants it packaged in a way that brings it closer to the finished products and tropes of research reporting and away from the living presence of participative experience.

In response to this challenge, many participatory projects try to understand participation not in a third-person way, as a form of social practice, but in a first-person way as a form of *experience,* which orients to intersubjective relations and acknowledges the multiplicity of first-person positions. The participatory nature of the enquiry in participatory projects is characterized by an openness, a reflexive questioning approach, which distinguishes it from projects that have been designed to validate and confirm already established knowledge. This commitment to openness is at the heart of design enquiry and it is pivotal to our argument about how participatory projects can function to create a step change in HCI, the field of its activity, and the relationships that constitute it.

Participatory Projects as Open Works

Participatory projects can be open works in a number of different ways. There is a very basic sense in which any participatory project, a key point of which is enquiry, has to be open to learning with and from others. To the extent that projects experiment with the conditions of participatory performance, other kinds of openness are brought into play, for example, structural openness to whatever subjective positions emerge in a participatory project. Finally, participatory projects can intentionally deploy questions, probes, or prototypes that are in one way or another incomplete or characterized by a tension that can only be resolved by the work of other participants. We found Umberto Eco's (1989) *The Open Work* particularly useful as we tried to work with the varieties of openness we encountered in participation.

According to Eco (1989), the idea of openness, and more particularly *open work*, provides an analytic resource to consider the space of relationships among artists, works of art, and audience. It draws attention to a classical model of reception of art and to variations of or movements away from that classical model. In the classical model, artists present a formally complete piece of work with the intention that it should be received and appreciated as they intended when composing it. However, each individual audience member brings his or her own experience and sensibilities to the work, the variety of interpretations adding something to its aesthetic value. The work is complete and closed as the uniquely composed piece that it is, nevertheless, at the same time being open in that it is subject to different interpretations. According to Eco, every reception of a work of art is an *interpretation* and a *performance* of it, because with every reception it takes on a different perspective. Eco's rendering of the classical model of reception as inherently open recognizes the active role played by audiences, whose attention amounts to tacit performance, bringing their creativity to seeing, listening to, or reading a work of art and, in the process, adding their voice to what becomes a polyvocal piece as audiences respond to it.

This dialogical model of tacit openness to the response of the audience points to an ineluctable participative quality of any engagement with a work, which we will develop as a starting assumption in our attempt to learn from participatory projects in the chapters that follow. It suggests questions, which we will pursue in these chapters, about the inevitability of participation; the potential for participation to be quiet, thoughtful, and deeply felt, even if not publicly played out; the values of a more explicit approach to participation in which the audience is encouraged to become performers (something already assumed in Eco's interpretive openness); and the relationships between researchers and participants in these projects as they unfold.

Many participatory projects are designed to explore more explicit forms of participative openness. Eco's (1989) essay also draws attention to such deliberate movements away from the classical model in the composition of works of art. One move involves authors or composers building in a form of interpretive openness by suggesting multiple, often metaphorical or analogical, meanings for their work. This idea of interpretive depth is often associated with, say, the writings of Shakespeare or biblical texts. Eco suggests that by employing this kind of openness the author makes available a limited set of interpretations but ultimately still keeps a degree of control over performance of the work in the sense that there is still a unique, complete, formally closed work to begin with.

Interpretive openness has been influential in the development of third-wave HCI and experience-centered design (Bødker 2006; Wright and McCarthy 2010). Sengers and Gaver (2006), starting with the question of whether all interactive systems are not to some extent interpretively open, describe how a more deliberate composed openness can be employed to engage users. They suggest that design for ambiguity can invoke curiosity and draw the user in to respond with their own interpretations. In interaction design, openness is a strategy for maximizing active engagement of users by inviting them to make sense of the ambiguity they encounter. Design for appropriation is another design strategy in which a system is designed to have sufficient flexibility to enable users to adapt to it in different ways to suit their own particular circumstances and modes of use. Although design for appropriation is a deliberate strategy, social studies of technology also abound with descriptions of systems that have been appropriated in ways that were not predicted at design time. In these cases, the designer essentially gives up control over how the work is received or used.

Sengers and Gaver (2006) explored interpretive openness, but other participatory projects are open in more tangible ways that resonate with Eco's discussion of *suggestive work* or *work in movement*. An open work of this type appears unfinished or structurally open, offering elements or building blocks for construction but leaving the final decision about exactly how to construct the piece up to the performer or audience. Eco gives examples of musical compositions in multiple sections, which the performer has to combine in any number of possible ways, novels in which a world is presented as always changing as it is perceived by the different characters at different times, and plays in which a particular point of tension is left to the audience to resolve. With particular reference to the plays, but applying in some measure to other examples too, Eco argues that "a solution is seen as desirable and is actually anticipated, but it must come from the collective enterprise of the audience" (1989, 11).

In these forms of openness there is no single position for the spectator. Instead, this kind of work "induces the spectator to shift his position continuously in order to see the work in constantly new aspects, as if it were in a state of transformation" (Eco 1989, 7). In these projects, the spectator is expected to be creatively responsive to the work of art. In some open work, an inexhaustible range of possible meanings is supported, because the world of the work is driven by ambiguity "both in the negative sense that directional centres are missing and in a positive sense, because values and dogma are consistently being placed into question" (Eco 1989, 9). We have already referred to projects in chapter 1 that were deliberately designed as unfinished requiring the participants to actively engage in the coproduction of content (in the case of StoryBank) and of structure and behavior (in the case of Open Burble). In later chapters, other forms of explicit openness that require participants to work with multiple positions and transformations are discussed, for example, in BOSOP (chapter 4), Jacob House and the Women's Centre (both chapter 5), and others.

Some participatory projects explore public participation by using technically and culturally open social media platforms. The participative experience of becoming in publics is something to which we will return in chapter 6. For now, a brief example will indicate the potential for participatory publics created by the continuing emergence of social media. Urban Remix uses a social media platform to enable participants to create a work in movement but also to form a community of users and an ongoing participation that lives beyond the individual performance events. The Urban Remix platform consists of a mobile phone system and a web interface for recording, browsing, and mixing audio so that participants become active creators of shared soundscapes. They use their mobile phones to collect sounds, voices, and noises of the city. They then record those sounds on the website as an original soundtrack that can be browsed and mixed to create a soundscape that expresses their idea of the acoustic identity of their community. Urban Remix is not just a performance event; rather, it is more like a participatory platform. The public can upload sounds and create journeys at any time. They can also run projects that bring people together to participate in joint projects that are archived.

We started this section with the aim of defining commitment to openness as one of the defining characteristics of participatory projects. A review of conceptualizations of open work by Eco and by Sengers and Gaver has shown that openness is a multilayered construct. At one level, we have seen that every work, and perhaps all cultural artifacts including interactive systems, is effectively open to a wide range of possible readings and appropriations, which gives the work new vitality with each particular act of engagement with it. At a second level, those open works in which the author hands something like resources to performers are characterized by the invitation to *make* the work together with the author, when making the work entails some combination of composing, assembling, and controlling. At a third level, the author constructs platforms that effectively scaffold the participants to create, compose, and perform their own works.

This multilayered conceptualization of openness suggests that different forms of participation yield different answers to questions about the configuration of social relations in participation. As well as seeing participatory projects as design enquiries into participative experience, the openness of participatory enquiry is seen as plural and layered. It is not a matter of the work being open or not, but of how and when it is open and whether that openness has been deliberately designed. Open work that is handed as a resource by author to performer poses a question to designers trying to create participative experience. Sengers and Gaver's reflections on ambiguity and appropriation in interaction design led them to wonder whether it is ever valuable to enforce and encourage a single, consensual interpretation and, if so, how and when? The question for them is *when* is it appropriate for the designer to take control of the interpretive process and when is it appropriate and even necessary for the designer to relinquish control of the interpretive process? Recognition of this possibility unsettles starting assumptions about designer-user relations.

Participatory Projects as Reconfiguring Social Relations

The previous section makes the point that participation in HCI does not entail an unquestioned commitment to openness. It argues that the researcher has to think critically about whether and where openness becomes a feature of the project. What should be shared and what should be held back? What roles should people be given and what should be allowed to emerge? Thinking this way about openness leads to the need to consider how participation is configured in these participatory projects: what roles people play, how those roles are sometimes reconfigured as part of the enquiry, why new roles might emerge, and even how technology can be used to sustain existing configurations in a changing world. In this section, we consider three approaches to reconfiguring social relations in participation. The first involves temporary experiments in reconfiguring relationships in performance. The second involves relationships between researchers and participants as they emerge in real world engagements and how they are reconfigured in different contexts. The third involves building platforms that support the emergence and growth of new configurations and forms of participation beyond the project.

Temporary Experiments in Reconfiguring Relationships in Performance

A number of fairly experimental projects have explored aspects of how social relationships are configured in participation. For example, a series of experiments on performance in mixed-reality street games explored the social contract that develops between performers and spectators, how this helps them to understand not only the conventions involved in taking part but also what happens as the game unfolds (Benford et al. 2006). In the Humanaquarium project, which will be discussed in some detail in chapter 3, researchers explore the facilitators and inhibitors of participation in a musical performance in which the research team are also the musical performers. Members of the audience make a situated and public movement from being an audience member to being a performer, which for some is experienced as quite challenging. In this section, we will focus on one specific experiment in which participation in musical performance is arranged over the Internet.

Atau Tanaka is a digital music composer, performer, and researcher. In his exploration of the expressive potential of digital instruments, the participation of listeners in the creative process as producers of content has become a focus of some of his projects. Tanaka sees concerns such as engagement, sociability, improvisation, mutuality, and turn taking as directly pertinent to music making and, in this context, presents a collaboration that leads to jointly produced meaning or the creation of shared interpretation, resonant of musical performance and especially ensemble performance (Tanaka 2006).

Tanaka's exploration of a participatory aesthetics can be seen in his MP3q, a piece that uses open web browsing to enable visitors to contribute MP3 sound links to the MP3q system by simply sending a URL. MP3q then streams and mixes multiple channels of MP3 audio from servers on the Internet. On the MP3q browser, users can manipulate and mix streams of audio. In a very tangible way, listeners create the musical material of a piece in MP3q. MP3q presents listeners with a space of possibilities and largely leaves how to proceed in that space up to the listeners. They contribute, manipulate, and mix the sounds.

In Eco's terms, MP3q is a *work in movement* but it seems to us to go further than Eco's description. In *work in movement,* the composer would produce a score that includes instructions to play the files randomly or in the order of the player's choice. MP3q goes a step further by having no score. The composer does not produce or work with a musical score or give anything like a musical score to the listeners, who become performers, leaving even more substantive aspects of authorship and performance open to the listener-performer. In MP3q, the role of composer is also distributed, with the audience at least in part composing and assembling the piece that the members also perform.

In contrast to conventional understandings of musical performance, Tanaka situates individual listeners as creative contributors in a collective musical performance. As is the case with Haque's Open Burble (Haque 2010), the designer-composer creates a situation in which there are clear channels for participants to contribute creatively. Haque and Tanaka design open systems in which nothing happens; there is no performance or event until participants interact with the instruments that the designers have made available to them. Both explore the conditions for dialogue and aesthetic experiences and the possibility that a dialogical encounter between people and technology, and between individual and collective, can be an aesthetic experience. But where Haque and Tanaka differ, at least in these projects, is in the amount of structure that is given to the audience-participant. With MP3q, audience-performers are given little by way of Eco's "components of a construction kit"; rather, they are given something that might be more appropriately described as a platform on which to build and a medium in which to work.

The primary purpose of reconfiguring the audience response in these temporary experiments is to offer an aesthetic experience that the participants would not be able to achieve without the technology; the technology enables a temporary reconfiguration in which an audience member can become a performer for a while and a performer can experience new forms of improvisation.

Reconfiguring Designer-User Relations Longer Term

One of the major challenges to participatory projects is an inertia in institutions, communities, and individuals that resists openness and dialogical enquiry, preferring to work with well-established and understood boundaries. Sometimes this is through lack of realization that other configurations of projects are possible, sometimes because reconfigurations threaten existing power structures, sometimes through lack of time and effort, and sometimes because of fear of the unknown. Nevertheless participatory projects are predicated on the idea of reconfiguration of traditional roles, and a diverse range of approaches to achieving dialogue are explored in the projects described in this book.

In the Personhood project, what could have been configured as a formal relationship between an informant and a researcher soon became the beginnings of a friendship. Friendships by their definition are mutual and reciprocal and they represent one of the most trusting forms of relationship. They are often nurtured by sharing experiences and building memories together, and through this they establish mutual empathy for each other's needs and goals. *Friendship* seems at first glance to be a word more associated with domestic and private life than the world of research, design, and business. But, of course, most people's experiences of the workplace and even with business negotiations is that the best collaborations are between people who not only sit around a committee room table together but also a dinner table and even a bar table.

In chapter 5 we describe a number of participatory projects, which have taken place in institutions such as care homes and women's centers. The experience of researchers here seems to be that entering the field is a particularly important part of the invitation to participate and the way in which trust is established. In these settings, researchers found that configuring themselves as university researchers was not always helpful for building trusting relationships. The concepts of university and research were alien to most of participants in the institutions, including the staff. There was no common ground or basis for empathy and relationship building, and it was hard to resist the configuration of university researchers as "studying and scrutinizing us" or "trying to teach us." Researchers in several of these projects undertook instead to do an initial period of voluntary work or casual visits within the institutions. They became familiar faces, they had a clear role of value to the institution, and they began to be trusted as people, not just university researchers. During this phase of volunteering they did not disguise the fact they were university researchers or that they might have an interest in doing some research, but they did not interview, take notes, or document this processes.

In another project described in chapter 3, the institutional context was a medium-secure women's forensic ward, where access to the women was difficult because of issues of safety and well-being of the researcher and the women. In this situation the researcher did much of the preliminary work with members of staff acting as a kind of proxy for the women but also providing invaluable expertise on the issues the researcher would face. Only later in the project did the researcher meet with the women for whom she was designing, a process that was configured by the staff.

An Aspiration toward a Project Legacy

The projects we discuss are generally relatively short-term research projects that have funding for three years or so to work on a specific issue. Their capacity to leave a lasting legacy is limited by these institutional arrangements and by their need to give priority to traditional research outputs. Nonetheless many of these projects have a concern for the long-term consequences of their work and a desire to make a lasting difference, to make something that matters to someone. In participatory projects the nature of what matters to people is often diverse and complex.

In projects such as MP3q, the aspiration for legacy for the public audiences may be simply that people have fun together in an unusual and hopefully memorable way. But also perhaps the aspiration is for people to participate in a technological imaginary in which they not only encounter a musical performance that enables them to see themselves and their capabilities a little bit differently but also empowers them to explore new forms of creative play in a space of possibilities. For the performers and designers, the legacy is more tangible in terms of academic research and also in terms of an ongoing investigation into, and learning about, the potential of digital interactive systems to create new forms of creative expression.

In other projects we shall describe in this book, there is an aspiration to leave behind the technology that was developed during the project. The Prayer Companion project (described in chapter 5) left behind the technology that they designed for an enclosed order of nuns. The Prayer Companion, a small T-shaped, crosslike object, displays news headlines and short statements about personal feelings taken from social media sites in response to the nuns' desire to have their prayer life informed by some knowledge of what was going on in the outside world. The Photostroller project (also described in chapter 5) developed a device that shows a slideshow of photographs retrieved from Flickr for residents of a care home for older people to facilitate their engagement in the wider social and physical world beyond the care home, and this was also left behind. These devices have now been with the communities for a number of years.

For some projects, a legacy is a far more ambitious thing and one that can be fraught with ethical and political problems akin to those seen in development projects, such as StoryBank. Such projects sometimes seek to transform lives in a lasting way. We need to be careful about the word *transformation* in this context. It accurately reflects what participatory projects can and do bring about but it may not be as dramatic as the ballyhoo surrounding notions that transformation and transformative experience may suggest. The Bespoke project was ambitious in wanting to make a lasting impact in Callon and Fishwick, an area of high unemployment, deprivation, and social exclusion in the north of England. The aim of the project was to explore factors that create social exclusion and exclusion from the digital economy of a neighborhood. The project also aimed to work with local activist-led projects to revitalize Callon and Fishwick. Community journalism and bespoke design were used to enable the community to create novel ways of meeting their needs and to help revitalize the area.

During the project, various technologies were deployed in the communities. As part of the handover at the end of the project, the hosts of these devices were invited to retain them. However, in contrast to the Photos-troller and Prayer Companion projects mentioned previously, the hosts of these devices asked for them to be removed. They saw them as taking up too much space and not providing a service that was of value to the ven-ues, and despite the team's best intentions, the systems were not used by the community after the project ended and all installations were removed within six months of the end of the project. The Bespoke team members went on to examine the practical challenges of leaving a technological legacy (Taylor et al. 2012), drawing attention to the need to ensure that usage is self-sustaining before the end of a project and any attempt to hand over the technologies involved. Their suggestions include the importance of building local expertise before the project ends.

But perhaps more important for Bespoke, local groups and individuals who had been involved in the project have since become involved in sub-sequent projects with members of the research and design team. Perhaps most encouragingly, elements of the journalism service that was developed have continued to operate in the community (Taylor et al. 2013).

In many of the projects described later, these social reconfigurations and the lasting relationships that result are at least as important a legacy as the technology that gets left behind. In the case of the Personhood project, this took the form of a friendship, and the technological legacy was something more of a gift that symbolized that relationship. In others there may be no technological legacy at all and the relationship may not be as intense as friendship; there may simply be a willingness for both sides to do some-thing together again. For others the legacy may be even less tangible: it may be simply be new ways of looking and a new perspective. These may not be limited to technology but may extend to understanding better each other's particular expertise, values, and commitments.

Taken together this sketch of four themes—design enquiry, openness, reconfiguration, and legacy—provide us with a starting idea of the scope of participatory projects, and with some qualities and questions to be exam-ined in the chapters that follow. Before we move onto those chapters, we need to explore a second concept through which we have structured this exploration: the concept of genres of participation.

Genres of Participation

Up to this point, we have defined some of the key elements and spaces for a conceptual framework for participatory projects and some of the ques-tions and issues raised in consideration of those spaces. These concepts could already constitute a critical framework for participatory practice. They could be used to explore the potential of participatory projects in HCI. However useful though that would be, it would lack a perspective on the aims of designers when they initiate these projects and on the social and cultural contexts in which they set these projects. Although there is coherence in the category *participatory projects,* it should not be imagined as referring to a homogenous flat space in which all projects operate at the same level, on the same topics and issues, with the same interests. In an attempt to capture that variation, we describe four genres of participatory project in the next four chapters. *Genre* is a more suitable word than *type* or *form* or *class* because the distinctions we have in mind for participatory projects are quite organic, culturally sensitive, and resist being finalized. When we think of genres in areas such as film or music, they tend not to be precisely definable, subject to change over time and situation, and amenable to modification or renewal through fusion, borrowing, or recombining, often a result of individual creativity pushing the boundaries of a genre. John Seely Brown and Paul Duguid (1996) use the example of the tension between tradition and innovation in jazz to make a point about the permeability of genre boundaries:

In jazz, for instance, Miles Davies claimed that Wynton Marsalis was too respectful of old forms to go anywhere new. Other musicians, however, criticized Davis for moving too far beyond the conventional forms to be understood. Almost every time that he moved across musical boundaries, Davis was charged with incoherence.... Before long, however, it usually became apparent that he had built a new audience for his work, and a new frontier for musicians—often led by Davis himself—to cross. (Brown and Duguid 1996, 142)

Designers often push against boundaries and conventions. This is particularly true in participatory projects, which in their commitment to openness certainly push against convention and tradition. So genre is a useful means of describing variety among these projects without implying that projects are defined by their genres or indeed can belong to one genre only. Crossover is a recognized feature of many cultural forms including design convention.

Genre has been defined in many different ways, for example, in terms of similarities in style, form, strategy, situation, or audience. Approaches to genre that identify an aspect of performance around which the differences between genres are defined risk reduction, formalism, "critical determinism of the worst kind" (Patton 1976, cited in Miller 1984, 151) and "tiresome and useless taxonomies" (Conley 1979, cited in Miller 1984, 151). In their place, Miller (1984) sees genre "as a recurrent, significant action ... [that]

... embodies an aspect of cultural rationality" (Miller 1984, 165), a way of "going on" that embodies deep cultural understanding.

For example, film genres such as documentary and fiction can be understood as culturally meaningful social action. In broad terms, filmmakers and audiences understand the aims and conventions of both and engage with each other through a mutual appreciation of that cultural information. The history of the documentary is in social realism and public service. In the historical context of 1930s Britain, the point of documentary films was to offer a social service for dealing with problems of national importance (Turner 1988). In this context British documentary films developed a grim, gritty realist aesthetic that conveyed the weight of the work they were intended to do during very hard times. Documentary audiences appreciate the genre as an aesthetically sensitive way of informing, affecting, and activating. Filmgoers are likely also to appreciate the influence that the wartime documentary aesthetic had on postwar filmmaking, especially in Britain. From the 1950s on, the grainy realism of the British documentary was carried over into feature films and television, enabling these mediums to convey the social reality of the poverty and violence of postindustrial cities in films such as *This Sporting Life* and TV series such as *Boys from the Blackstuff*. At around the same time, the neorealist movement in postwar Italian filmmaking adopted a grainy underlit look, played down narrative, often replaced actors with real people to make film more true to life, and depended less on contrived structuring devices. It could be argued that in more recent times, the direction of influence has been the other way around with US documentaries on political corruption, climate change, and corporate greed borrowing feature film tropes to engage and entertain audiences, as well as inform and activate them. Documentary, fictional feature films, and television have coevolved these methods for "going on" and making the next film, in which new approaches are developed by finding new ways of looking at existing dialogical practices. Seen this way, genres are dialogical resources that evolve with use and participate in shaping cultural rationalities.

Adopting this approach enables us to see genres of participatory projects as recurring, meaningful, dialogical patterns of going on with others in particular cultural contexts that coevolve with use. Miller (1994) clarified that the cultural contexts in which genres took shape as forms of social action were best seen as rhetorical communities, something that sits very well with the final genre we discuss in chapter 6, *participating in publics*.

The first genre, which will be discussed in chapter 3, centers on *understanding the other*. The cultural context in projects such as Open Burble and Humanaquarium is the staged event or performance in which people engage with each other for a limited period of time to express themselves, have fun, share an experience with others, or enjoy and join in with the experience evoked by that particular performer. Although these events are temporally and spatially bounded from the public's point of view, from the designer's point of view each performance may be one of a series of encounters with different members of the public through which the designed performance, experience, or artifact is refined. This genre is often invoked in participatory projects to enquire into the dynamics of public participation in performance and at times to *reconfigure participation* in that context, too.

The Personhood project exemplifies the second genre, which will be discussed in chapter 4. This genre is characterized by *building personal relationships* and evokes extended encounters that occur over months and even years. The cultural context is the long-term relationship in which people get to know each other well over time during which they show interest in each other's experiences, feeling, hopes, and well-being. This genre is invoked in participatory projects that focus on people's lived experience and on enabling people's voices to be heard in the ongoing encounter between designers and participants often during design and generally in making artifacts and acting with and through them.

In chapter 5, a third genre concerned with *belonging in community* is discussed. This includes projects that treat community as a given and explore the roles that technology can play in communities, and projects that focus on the process of participation by looking at diversity and the sense of wanting to belong in community. The cultural context here is socially engaged practice, which can be seen in community art, publicly supported community initiatives, and community activism. It involves a sustained encounter over a period of time between members of the community and those artists, workers, or activists who may come from outside or within the community, whose aim is to catalyze change. Participatory practices that resonate with this genre focus on guiding and facilitating action to reconfigure social relations in the site of intervention.

With the significant growth of engagement with social media, the fourth genre, *participating in publics,* which is discussed in chapter 6, is an increasingly salient participatory genre. For many commentators, publics developed around social media are the defining characteristic of the participatory cultures of our time. This is an emerging cultural context in which dialogical patterns of going on together in rhetorical communities are still forming, and as such it provides participatory projects with an opportunity to observe the autopoetic realization of some of the practices they aim for in their design-led enquiries. It also points to what will surely be an important future strand of participatory projects in HCI and an important aspect of future interaction, too.

Toward a Critical Dialogue

Participatory projects represent the most recent manifestation of a participatory technological imaginary that stretches back at least a century and that finds expression in many aspects of contemporary participatory culture including science, health, and entertainment. Practice and discourse in areas such as participatory development and arts have informed our view on participatory projects in HCI. In each of these areas, people who take the initiative to engage in an activity or project believe that their contributions matter and feel a degree of connectedness to each other. Although it is relatively straightforward to describe the broad character of the participatory in contemporary culture, the lack of a critical dialogue about the range of forms of participation that are available makes it far more difficult to systematically understand and evaluate practice and discourse in the area.

In chapters 1 and 2 we have cleared some ground that enables us to appreciate the value and potential of participative experience in HCI. Throughout we have emphasized the dialogical in participative experience, the sense of reflexive engagement and communication with others that entails potential for change in how we see ourselves and the world around us. From this perspective participatory projects bring about the potential for people to see themselves in a variety of positions, for example, as composer, maker, and controller, author producer, and actor, all of which are defined in terms of their relationships to others in the project and the situations brought about through the project. In terms of the development of a critical dialogue about the practices and discourses of participatory projects, recognition of this potential inevitably raises questions about the particular positioning of participants in any individual project and the extent to which they are treated as differently placed centers of value who can contribute to shaping their own futures. In HCI, these questions can more generally be applied to relationships between designers and users. They can also be applied to the relationship between participants and technology and the extent to which that relationship describes an architecture that is dynamic, responsive, and conversant.

Consistent with a dialogical approach, we have also emphasized enquiry as a primary focus of participatory projects. Moreover, given that these projects are concerned with participative experience, we have highlighted their participative, affective, and discursive elements of enquiry. Exploration of participative experience can be facilitated by a participative methodology in which the relationship between experience and one's sense of agency in that experience is focal and perhaps a defining quality of some projects. In some, participation becomes a way of living in and enquiring about the world and an ethic and aesthetic for design enquiry. Highlighting participative design enquiry as a possible approach indicates a space in which to discuss the epistemology, aesthetics, and ethics of design enquiry. At the center of this space is the particular of lived experience and at the margins is theoretical abstraction. A focus on lived experience avoids getting bogged down in trying to identify mental (theoretical) constructs and instead enables all participants to attend to the spontaneity of dialogical moments, which make practices visible as a point from which to go on.

Also consistent with a dialogical approach, and in some cases as a requirement for participatory design enquiry, there is a strong commitment to openness in participatory projects. Their openness can often be positioned at the far end of a continuum from the interpretive openness of all cultural artifacts where work is deliberately designed to be open. As well as considering the position of individual projects in this space, as part of contextualizing them and the dialogical moments they make possible, a critical dialogue should include the related issue of what is called in participatory art "the politics of spectatorship" (Bishop 2012). Although the imaginative capacity and courage to create and deploy unfinished work is admirable, questions about where it leaves spectators (and indeed creators) in performance remain open. In HCI, what values inform an interaction design that deliberately leaves work unfinished for users? Whose interests and needs are being satisfied and how? What kind of relationship among designers, makers, and users is enacted in these projects and why? Is there a chance, as some working in international and rural development provocatively suggest, that a participatory impulse can become institutionalized as a tyranny of participation?

Some projects make open work as an intriguing design enquiry about participative experience. Some perform experiments in staged performance settings. Others also contribute to reconfiguring participation by suggesting to all concerned a redistribution of roles in design, making, and appropriation. This suggests another multilayered space for dialogue. Many of those projects also intend to leave a legacy by reconfiguring the social in the sites in which they are active, for example, reconfiguring social relations by ensuring that participants have a voice in them and by leaving behind technologies that mediate social relations. A critical dialogue has to address this political aspect of participatory projects, too.

3 Understanding the Other

This chapter addresses a number of themes related to engaging members of the public in participatory projects. As we have already seen in Open Burble (Haque 2010), MP3q (Tanaka 2006), and StoryBank (Frohlich et al. 2009), participation can involve serious commitment on the part of members of the public who take part. Yet, as we will consider in detail in chapter 6, commitment notwithstanding, huge numbers of people voluntarily participate in self-organizing social media publics. We will leave social media participation to chapter 6 and concentrate in this chapter on the kinds of projects in which researchers guide people to take part with others, often in public events. These projects can take time and an emotional commitment to putting oneself on the line in front of friends, peers, or even a public audience.

Researchers who organize participatory projects are generally aware of the challenges for participants and look for ways in which taking part might be rewarding for them, from trying to minimize the emotional costs to trying to make sure that taking part will be a satisfying creative experience. Public staged events—musical performance, role-play, and community theater—provide a useful model for exploring the potential for participation in HCI. They often involve finding ways of encouraging members of the public, who would typically be passive members of an audience at, say, a musical performance, to take part actively in making the music. This approach involves reconfiguring participation by enabling people to change roles from the ones they would habitually perform. Other approaches assume that people listening to and responding to the same music are already actively participating and that the research challenge is to make that participation sensible or visible.

In a published conversation about his public space installations, the British sculptor Antony Gormley makes a distinction that roughly corresponds with the difference between the two approaches just outlined (Gormley 2008). Gormley distinguishes what he describes as explicit or "loud" participation and implicit or "quiet" participation. In *explicit participation*, the ostensible activity of participation is an explicit focus of the project. Audience participation is often staged in a theatrical manner, such as members of the audience moving through the space of performance to take a part. This will be seen in some of the projects described in the following in which audience members move to the stage to become performers. In contrast, *implicit participation* is quiet and internal, a subliminal sense one has of taking part in something that links "the inner life of the spectator … to a wider field" (Gormley 2008). In implicit participation, members of the public, on encountering the conditions within a space created by an artist, "become aware of [their] being through a different frame" (Gormley 2008). This can be seen in projects in which the artist creates or changes a situation to prompt people in that space to see it, and their position in it, in a new way. It is a particular way of making quiet participation sensible.

Making participation sensible will be a recurring theme that we will introduce in this chapter. Starting with a commitment to making participation sensible leads to a variety of forms of participation that go beyond role switching (e.g., audience members becoming performers for a while).

Central to the commitment to participation as a value in HCI projects and to the pragmatics of making it happen is concern for the other. It seems to us that most research in this area involves empathic concern for others, in its cognitive, imaginative, and affective dimensions and that that empathy informs the conceptualization of many projects and the practicalities of making them happen. Empathy is often thought of as a relation between people who are already familiar but in the projects we discuss it finds immediate expression in encounters with strangers.

Encounters with Strangers

Encountering the other evokes the idea of meeting and coming to terms with difference. Etymologically, encounter has its origins in the Latin word *contra*, which means *against*, suggesting opposition or conflict. The word does bear a broader definition though, from meeting with an opponent to meeting with someone different or a stranger. The phrase *encountering the other* is intended here to carry that broader sense of meeting and coming up against otherness, strangeness, people and worlds that are different. As a genre of participatory project, encountering the other is an experiment with the pleasure and imagination of engaging with something new.

According to the anthropologist Julie Cruikshank (2005), encounters produce local knowledge and social imagination. For her, an encounter is an engagement that involves coming upon something different or strange—a stranger, a novel situation, a different knowledge tradition—and having to make sense of it. She draws attention to how accommodating imbalances in knowledge between participants (e.g., the local person knowing how to manage a difficult situation in ways that the visiting professional does not) influences how all participants imagine each other and interpret their relationship. For Cruikshank, it is in this process of making sense of situations and experiences with others who have different stories and perspectives that local knowledge and social imaginaries are produced. But, as Cruikshank notes, encounters do not guarantee understanding; they sometimes make clear what is incommensurate.

The idea that learning and imagination are produced in encounters with others draws on an understanding of human development that emphasizes social experience in learning and creativity. In *Technology as Experience* (McCarthy and Wright 2004), following Bakhtin, Vygotsky, Dewey, and others, we argued that it is through encounters with others that we come to know ourselves. When two people meet in dialogue, they bring different personal histories and experiences, skills, and perspectives on the world to the encounter. This gives each of them what Bakhtin calls a *surplus of vision* with respect to the other. By this he meant that each person could see the other in ways that the other cannot see him- or herself. This surplus of vision imbues the encounter with a creative potential and learning that does not otherwise exist (Wright and McCarthy 2010). In dialogical encounters, participants may act in accordance with each other's expectations or they might do something unexpected, creating new ways of seeing and new understanding. Dialogical encounters of this sort construct situations in which people experience a sense of the value of another person, and learn about self and other, not only as they are now but also as they might be in the future. In short, the dialogical encounter is replete with possibilities for development and change.

The projects that we explore in this chapter owe something to the earlier emergence of practices and discourses in participatory arts, in which, for example, those usually positioned as spectators are invited to become artists, performers, or makers, for a time, to stimulate creativity or raise awareness. The idea is that enabling people to step out of their habitual situations and roles encourages them to see other ways of being and to reflect on their own modes of experiencing. One of the main things we learn from the participatory arts is that there are many ways of enabling people to explore new ways of taking part.

One aesthetic response, as we saw when discussing Eco's open work in chapter 2, reenvisions the artwork as a construction kit for performers and for members of the public. *Happenings* go a step further by ensuring that everybody participates. They are organized activities that "select[s] and combine[s] situations to be participated in, rather than watched or just thought about" (Kaprow 2003, 87). *Happenings* depend quite a lot on chance encounters between participants with vague guidelines given to performers to relate their activity to the surrounding props. Whereas Eco's open works are generally staged in traditional artistic performance settings with fairly clear guidelines for participants, *Happenings* experiment with free-form participative activity in everyday contexts. Kaprow's *Happenings* in the early 1960s often involved taking friends or students to a specific site to perform a small action. Kaprow (2003) describes a number in his essay *Happenings in the New York Scene* (1961), including the following one: "Everybody is crowded into a downtown loft, milling about, like at an opening. It's hot. There are lots of big cartons sitting all over the place. One by one they start to move, sliding and careening drunkenly in every direction, lunging into one another, accompanied by loud breathing sounds over four loudspeakers." The context is a small group, typically including Kaprow, interacting in some unspecified way with an event that is happening in fairly basic everyday surroundings. There is no plot and everything that happens involves improvisatory response to the situation and actions, playing with chance and spontaneity. These events were rarely recorded, making them one-off performances in which the action, the participative experience, and the "happening" that occurred was the point. Bishop (2011) describes a contrasting aesthetic with which she associates the Moscow-based Collective Actions Group (CAG). CAG was active from the mid-1970s during the communist era. In contrast to Kaprow's *Happenings*, their practice positions the conversations that take place after the encounter as the aesthetic point. Contrasting it with the primacy of the immediate experience of the encounter in *Happenings*, Bishop emphasizes personal reflection and participation in discussion after the event as the site in which experience is made meaningful and subject positions developed.

Although there is a query implied in this contrast about when meaning is made—in the action or in the dialogue afterward—we have previously argued that lived experience does not carve life up so neatly, and that anticipation, activity, reflection, and sharing are all implicated in sense making. Different sociopolitical contexts (New York in the 1960s and Moscow in the 1970s) favor different approaches to configuring participation. In one context, talk, debate, and documentary may be cheap, and in another it may be very hard won and insistently participative. Both play with the relationship between individual and collective experience and with the distribution of the sensible that can shape how people perceive and participate in particular configurations.

Redistributing the Sensible: Introducing Rancière

The distribution of the sensible is a key idea in Jacques Rancière's writing on aesthetics and politics, how they inhere in each other, and how participation in the social world is influenced by what is sensible. Here *sensible* refers to what can be apprehended by the senses and therefore the idea that there is a distribution of the sensible draws attention to divisions between what is visible and invisible, sayable and unsayable, audible and inaudible, thinkable and unthinkable. It acts as a reminder that in any social situation some things can be thought, made, and done, and others cannot. Analysis of how modes of participation are influenced by modes of perception in the distribution of the sensible is the part of Rancière's work that is most relevant to our consideration of participation. However, understanding the phrase and its potential in our discussion of encountering the other in participation may be helped by understanding something of Rancière's philosophical position and method.

Rancière is a French philosopher who started as a structural Marxist as a student of Althusser's. He wrote *Reading Capital* with Althusser and others in 1968. However, after the 1968 student uprising in Paris, Rancière broke with Althusser. He argued that structural Marxism in general was elitist and lacking when it came to dealing with the students' activities. He accused it of not trusting spontaneous popular movements, such as the student movement, and of supporting a politics of order. He has since worked on a philosophy that values a variety of voices in a dissensual politics of emancipation. Rancière rejects ontological notions of politics as already always existing in preestablished interest groups or classes. For him, politics comes into being when somebody draws attention to the inequality in social order; when people who are excluded insist that their voices are heard, recognized, and responded to; when, by implication, people struggle to be heard in an established social order that deems what they have to say unsayable and what they want to discuss unthinkable.

Clearly, issues of exclusion and inclusion—being allowed to participate or being limited in how one is allowed to participate—are central to Rancière's dissensual politics of imagination. With the established social order founded on a distribution of the sensible that makes its rules common sense or unquestionable, it follows that the modes of participation available to people are determined by the modes of perception available. Politics comes into being when a struggle to be heard by people who are excluded challenges the existing social order and, when successful, brings about a reconfiguration of the distribution of the sensible. This close association between modes of participation and modes of perception in Rancière's work ensures that aesthetics (broadly understood as an enquiry into the sensible) and politics (as struggle to reconfigure the sensible) are interdependent.

Rancière's work can be seen as a series of interventions in particular areas such as education, workers' history, and aesthetics, each of which asks how that area becomes political. He draws attention to the ways in which the polemical in each of his areas of interest (work, art, pedagogy) makes it an object of thinking and situates it in a field of tensions (Bowman and Stamp 2011). Instead of developing an ontology of politics, education, or aesthetics, he draws attention to how the subject of each comes into being only when an inequality is named, for example, not being heard and responded to, in any of these areas. It is at that point, he argues, that the accepted order of things is shown to be a policed order, controlling what is sensible. This *distribution of the sensible* allocates roles and functions to people to keep order, and it depends on consensus. Questioning social order in any of these areas requires dissensus (Rancière 2010).

Dissensus is key to a critique of the possibility of emancipated participation that is promoted in much open work in art and in a number of movements in the participatory arts. Rancière (2009a), in a book called *The Emancipated Spectator,* argues that the kind of emancipation that is sought in a reconfiguration that makes spectators into performers in order to free them from the constraints of their "passive" role in the audience is better found in the assumption of equality in difference rather than in seeing equality as a goal. He argues that emancipation is not brought about by trying to make everybody the same but by starting from the assumption that all participants, though different from each other, are equal. Rancière's thesis suggests that members of an audience, students in a classroom and users in a participatory project, are all already active to the extent that they observe, select, interpret, integrate, critique, and imagine. They discuss the event afterward with friends and colleagues and share stories that help make sense of the experience for others. Seeing all of this as passive diminishes the cognitive and emotional in favor of the behavioral and, in the process, risks losing extremely important positionings in dialogue.

People observing, interpreting, and recounting from their particular positions are already transforming lived meaning. Moreover dialogue between people from their different perspectives has the potential to create something interesting and unexpected for both. This is Bakhtin's creative surplus, an emancipatory creativity that is best seen in terms of processes of interpreting and framing experience and existence, the freedom to go along with the role ascribed or to see things differently and use one's time differently to the way in which it seems to be ascribed. But beyond Bakhtin, Rancière's analysis adds two further ingredients to our understanding of the prerequisites for dialogue. The first is the shared assumption of equality in difference; the second is the commitment to learning as a mutual process of opening up new modes of perception for the people involved.

Instead of explicitly reconfiguring participation by encouraging people to change their positions, Rancière sees more potential for reconfiguration in the redistribution of the sensible, opening up new modes of perception and participation. Changing people's roles within a particular social organization without attending to the modes of perception that produced those roles in the first place merely reproduces the same social order with actors in different places. It's better to address the modes of perception and the distribution of the sensible. This resonates with Gormley's implicit approach to participation, in which people become aware of their being through encountering the conditions created in a particular space of performance.

To summarize, encountering the other involves experiencing strangers as well as challenging ways of being and knowing. Difficult though that may sound, encountering the other in participatory projects provides opportunities, often fun or stimulating opportunities, to try on new roles and reflect on experience in new situations. The creative surplus that is entailed in encountering the other and realizing the kinds of imbalances in knowledge and expertise that exist can also produce local knowledge and social imagination because accommodating to difference often requires an imaginative response. Seeing encounters as having that creative potential suggests lines of enquiry when considering specific participatory projects. These include questions reflecting on the framing of participation in these projects, for example, explicit theatrical events or quiet opportunities for reflection and action, as exercises in role reconfiguration or as enquiries into making the invisible visible in a particular setting and as concerned with particular aspects of participative experience (action, discussion, etc.) or as a more holistic approach to making sense in and of experience. Although an appreciation of the creative surplus in encountering another shapes our thinking on the potential of participatory projects, an appreciation of the distribution of the sensible in any project is key to understanding its value to (included and excluded) participants. Lest all of this begins to sound detached from the lived experiences of particular persons, as we approach specific projects we aim to enquire into the particular identities of those for whom something is sensible (or not) and those who have some say in making it sensible.

We start with a participatory musical performance, Humanaquarium, which is concerned with audience members taking on performer roles. It has an approach to reconfiguring social relations in participative performance, which is interactionally and socially more explicit for audience members than was the case in MP3q. It involves face-to-face contact between the research team (who are also the musical performers) and audience participants, who make a situated, public movement from being audience members to being performers, which for some is experienced as quite challenging. The affective cost of taking the initiative in Humanaquarium adds experiential complexity to the process of reconfiguration.

Empathic Encounters in Humanaquarium

Humanaquarium is a participatory musical event designed by Robyn Taylor and her colleagues. As well as experimenting with different ways of configuring participation, Taylor's work explores the affective and valuative aspects of participation such as performance anxiety, moral responsibility for participation, satisfaction and immersion. In Humanaquarium, the research team tries empathically to understand the experience of participation for members of the audience who take up the invitation to take part in the performance with a view to improving and scaffolding participative experience in performance. This is a connected form of enquiry that depends on keeping experience alive to find a way to participate in it or at least to engage imaginatively with it over time. Taylor and her colleagues call this *designing from within* the performance and use context (Taylor et al. 2011a).

The Humanaquarium (Taylor et al. 2011b) is a self-contained $1.5m^3$ cubic interactive performance space, in which a female soprano singer and a male accompanist perform. They are linked to a PA system outside of the cube and inside the cube they have musical equipment, including keyboards, microphones, mandolins, and laptop computers in front of them. The front face of the cube is a Perspex window that also acts as a touch screen. By gesturing on this touch screen, people outside the cube can control the parameters of the musical performance. The inside back face of the cube serves as a display surface for the projection of videos, graphics, and other animations. The light of the projector also illuminates the inside of the cube.

During a Humanaquarium performance, the two musicians perform in the cube, with projections cast onto the back wall, and a member or members of the audience interacting with the front-face touch screen. In this way, members of the audience effectively jam with the performers, collaboratively controlling the audiovisual content of each performance, and insofar as is technically possible, seeing the results of their actions. In addition, the third member of the team explicitly and implicitly (by demonstrating) encourages members of the audience to take part in the performance, and the performers respond in a social way to people who approach the box. The sensibility, informality, and approachability of the performance and the setting of the performance in places such as craft fairs, where people move around and are used to taking part in demonstrations, all contributed to a multilayered gesture of welcome and an invitation to participate in a performance, the "rules" of which were made as sensible as possible to the audience.

The Humanaquarium project was an open work in two senses. Not only was it completed by the audience during each performance but also it was completed by the designers over a series of performances, evolving during the lifetime of the project. Over the year or so spent living with the project, Humanaquarium was changed, redesigned, and modified on the basis of the accumulation of designers' experience of performing across venues and audiences. This design practice was not confined to spotting design problems and fixing them but constructing new understandings and new design spaces as the team made sense of their experiences of participation in performance. During performances, the performers could see that participants continued to experience some reticence about participating as audience-as-performer in Humanaquarium. The source of discomfort for participants still seemed to be the presence of other audience members.

The experience of simultaneously participating and observing was both intimate and anxiety provoking for the team. Two quotations from Taylor's thesis (Taylor 2012) illustrate the potential and the challenge of this approach. In the first, Taylor describes the performers' ability to see in intimate detail participants' interactions:

Schofield and I could see the faces of the participants through the acrylic window and were able to recount experiences and communications that were shared between ourselves and the participants as they watched one another through the glass. We were also uniquely positioned to observe smaller, more subtle communications and interactions between participants who had a perception of relative privacy when standing in front of the box with their backs to the observing audience. (104)

A couple of pages later, she describes the challenge of being both performing artist and observing designer:

From an artistic standpoint, this presented Schofield and I with a performance opportunity that was at once both exhilarating and anxiety-provoking—we were aware
that we would have to experience each participant-driven performance in a public
context (for better or for worse!) and use our artistry and professional skill to react to
participant behaviour truly on-the-fly in order to maintain the aesthetic integrity of
the public performance. (106)

The stance of the performer-designer in Humanaquarium is a reflexive
one. Their aim is not to observe the audience by standing apart from them.
Although they are looking through a Perspex screen, they are both looking
and being looked at, and what they do is affected by and affects the audience. They argue at the same time that neither are they aiming to imagine
themselves into the minds of the audience; rather, they are placing themselves within the experience but they are making sense of it from a different
point of view (as performers, designers, and experts). With this participative
method of enquiry, a high premium is placed on keeping the experience
of participating in performance alive by staying with the lived experience
rather than abstracting away from it.

By taking roles as performers within the interactive artworks, we are able to experience the effects of our design interventions first hand, accessing our own lived and
felt impressions of the shared experience. (Taylor 2012, 45)

The team also made video recordings of audience behaviors, they had colleagues in the audience take field notes, and they also carried out informal
conversations with audiences after the fact; reflective notes were taken at
the end of each performance and at the end of the series of performances.

Humanaquarium is an experiment in initiating and exciting participation in public performance. The research team sees the project as creating
new possibilities for aesthetic experience for themselves and for audience
members by reconfiguring social relationships through making alternative modes of participation sensible. Based on what they had learned from
participants in a previous experiments called dream.Medusa (Taylor et al.
2008), the team moved away from stage-based performance to performance
in the hall at craft fairs and other similar settings, and aimed to make the
relationship between actions and musical outcomes as apparent as possible
to participants. By positioning themselves within the performance, the
Humanaquarium performers (who are also its designers and researchers)
also make themselves visible to participants and audience members. Making themselves visible in this way, alongside the participants, makes the

quite complex set of roles and relationships sensible to everybody present. This is quite different from Open Burble and MP3q, in both of which design and researchers appear to be anonymous.

Participation in Humanaquarium involves face-to-face, almost body-to-body, copresence of performers and participants. As well as creating possibilities for making performance sensible to the audience, participation in Humanaquarium is an encounter that hopes to spark social imagination through dialogical engagement and empathic response. This started with a reflexive social response when participants approached the box, a response that was aware of the participant's vulnerability and the performers' needs. It continued with focused attention that looked at the participant from different perspectives, as we can see in some of the previous extracts, which show performers attending closely to the faces and the gestures of participants and micro-coordination occurring between performers and participants. This is an empathic response that is based in intellectual, emotional, and relational investments in the other's sense making, which opens up the potential for dialogical understanding. In encountering each other, performers and audience members learn from one other how different they are and what it takes to participate and to perform. In the encounter, the difference between performer and audience may well be made acutely sensible by feelings of vulnerability and stage fright on one side and feelings of anxiety about the performance on the other. Using a quieter, more implicit approach, Michael Asher's site-specific installations provide a reflective situation for visitors to art galleries and museums to encounter a variety of roles that are different to the role they would usually put on in these places.

Creating Dialogical Spaces—the Creative Potential of Difference

Michael Asher's site-specific installations trust the creative potential of difference. Asher was a conceptual artist who made temporary, site-specific installations in museums and galleries. Instead of trying to reconfigure participative roles and relations directly, Asher reframed situations in galleries and museums in which people usually encounter each other in a buttoned-down, constrained way. These installations evoke highly individuated encounters among visitors, gallery staff, and a variety of people contracted by Asher for specific projects. Some of Asher's work suggests ways in which participative encounters can result from the experience of difference when features of a gallery are changed in order to make difference sensible.

In one project, Asher removed the dividing walls between the gallery and the administration office in the Clare Copley Gallery in Los Angeles.

This created an uncanny experience for visitors having an unexpectedly personal, face-to-face encounter with the gallerist herself and the conditions in which she worked in her own gallery. Some visitors found this breach of preexisting social relations embarrassing and unsettling, which created the affective space for gallerist and visitors to enquire into and develop new insights about their social practices (Peltomäki 2010, 78). The conventional social contract is breached and a new contract has to be negotiated. As reported by Peltomäki (2010), one critic visiting the exhibition commented that

Standing directly in front of Copley ... it is almost impossible not to confront her and ask the inevitably embarrassing questions about the show. The viewer does not have the option of anonymously viewing the exhibition and leaving, nor can Copley feign ignorance of your presence. (Wortz, cited in Peltomäki 2010, 77)

Wortz's comment draws attention to the effect of Asher's installation on social relations in the Copley Gallery. Breaching the conventional divide between front of house and back of house, Asher makes the social and organizational processes of a gallery visible to all, perturbing the conventional approach to what can be seen and what can and should be spoken about in a gallery.

As Peltomäki points out, the psychological charge of the encounter between owner and critic in Copley's own gallery space—and we would add between visitors and a variety of contracted participants in other Asher projects—is the result of the emergence of new "affective economies" when prior social framings and cultural expectations have been perturbed. Following Sara Ahmed's arguments about affective economies, Peltomäki argues that the relationality of emotions shapes rather than reflects individual experience and identities. Ahmed's argument is that emotions do not reside in individual subjects or objects; rather, similar to aspects of economies, they circulate between subjects and objects. Ahmed sees this "nonresidence" of emotions as what enables them to mediate relationships between the individual and collective and to bind subjects together. In Asher's installations, the experience of viewing and the subjectivity of the viewer are produced in the social affective relations that prevail in the gallery. It is not so much that the boundary between visitor and gallery owner has been redrawn. Instead, it is that the particular emotions that circulate between them, given the unexpected visibility of difference, perturb the means of negotiating relationships and with that, the meaning of what it is to be gallery owner and critic. This enables us to see ways of reconfiguring participation by making difference sensible.

Asher's experiments open up the experience of participation and the work, including the emotional work, it involves. In so doing, they offer us a view into what it feels like to participate in an act of reconfiguration, a view from the inside as it were. By making alternative social configurations visible, Asher helps to create new possibilities for action and new ways of being through the intra-action of individuals in a given situation rather than a coming together of preexisting selves (Suchman 2007). As we have seen, this intra-action involves mediated encounters, a coming together of individuals with their own personal histories and expectations of the encounter, the experience of which is mediated by the emotions that circulate between them in the context of their difference and displacement. Asher's work also shows the creative potential of putting such difference in dialogue by making them visible in the encounter.

Similar issues have arisen in two participatory design projects on which one or both of us worked. In both projects the arrival of researchers and designers into a settled situation created an affective economy in which the meaning of the research and the role of researchers and designers, and even the means of negotiating those meanings and roles, had to be worked out emotionally and intellectually. One of the projects was carried out at Jacob House, a publicly funded residential care home in the north of England with about twenty-eight very elderly residents (Blythe et al. 2010). The majority of the residents were in their eighties and nineties when the fieldwork was done, the oldest was one hundred and four. This project is described in detail in chapter 5. In summary, the project was an extended ethnography in which a design team explored ways of encouraging the residents of Jacob House to engage in their community and to keep in touch with the world outside the home.

There is an important difference between the Jacob House project and the Copley Gallery installation. In the Copley Gallery, the situation ensured that visitors and gallerist experienced a sense of defamiliarization and a need to establish new ways of being in the gallery space. By contrast, in the Jacob House project, the researchers entered into someone else's space as strangers with a role (that of researcher) unfamiliar to the residents. Mark Blythe, who was carrying out fieldwork, found it extremely difficult to establish a role and identity for the residents. He visited the home regularly and in the first instance tried to engage the residents through "the normal ethnographic interview method" (Blythe et al. 2010, 1) but found that:

Residents were sometimes suspicious of the interviewer. They found interviews demanding, quickly became tired and sometimes distressed. For example, during an early interview with the hundred and four year old it was observed that she quite quickly became exhausted and upset *"Why are you asking me all these questions? Is it over now? I hope so!"* (Blythe et al. 2010, 162)

This difficulty was in part due to the age and circumstances of the residents but it was also due to the residents' lack of interest in performing as informant. Members of staff were also reluctant to participate at times, in part because of their suspicions about the researchers' true role:

The staff of residential care homes in the UK are inspected regularly and frequent media stories that feature undercover researchers make for a sense of constant surveillance. Some of the staff believed that the project researchers were something to do with the inspectors even though they were assured that this was not the case. It was not until a real inspection occurred during a research visit that all staff were finally convinced that the researchers were not something to do with the process. (Blythe et al. 2010, 163)

In the Spheres of Wellbeing project, Anja Thieme and colleagues (2013) worked with vulnerable psychiatric patients in a forensic hospital to explore ways in which digital technologies could support their dialectical behavior therapy. The patients were women with a dual diagnosis of borderline personality disorder and learning disability and they lived in a medium-secure unit of the hospital. The women's participation in the project was mediated by a long collaborative engagement between the research team and the staff of the unit. The staff involved were clinically trained and research oriented. One, the research and development manager, was a cognitive and behavioral therapist and had worked in the women's services in that capacity for a number of years. Another, a staff nurse, was interested in the research project as part of a master's degree. Staff participation in this project was crucial for a number of reasons. They helped the research team understand the clinical, safety, and security issues. They also played a useful role in immersing the research team in a service during a period in which engagement with the women was restricted due to the extended ethical and organizational preparation needed. However, this was far from simply a bureaucratic engagement because the staff was instrumental in shaping design ideas. For example, the personal safety and security of staff, patients, and the researchers was a primary concern for the staff and these discussions influenced the choice of materials. Equally, discussions about the nature of patients' learning disabilities influenced the choice of very visual, practical, and versatile physical forms. Working with these and other concerns about personalization and identity, Anja and her colleagues developed the design concept of spheres, a descriptive label for the design spaces to be explored with the women.

In the final phase of the research the women were invited to join the designers in workshops to help develop personalized interactive artifacts, personalized spheres. The women used art and crafts materials to create pieces that appealed to them. The creative activities facilitated tangible participation as well as enabling the women to learn skills and recognize their own strengths in a calm creative atmosphere. The one- to two-hour sessions were held in the women's familiar environment to reduce any anxiety they might experience during the activities. For the women, the workshops presented a quite exceptional participative experience. Because of their classification as secure patients, they would not usually be allowed to work with someone from outside the hospital staff team or allowed to handle objects such as pencils and knifes that could be used as weapons. For Anja it presented not only a unique opportunity but also an extremely challenging one. She was required to receive personal training on how to conduct herself safely during the workshops. This included restriction on where she should position herself around the table in relation to the women in order to be safe. All equipment used in the workshops had to be counted in and counted out and managed safely during the sessions. A member of staff had to be present at all times to check that the women were not becoming distressed, agitated, or aggressive and at risk of self-harm or harming Anja. During the sessions Anja worked nonjudgmentally to recognize and respond to the women's interests, abilities, and needs and helped the women to work with the various materials to create personalized content that appealed to them (Thieme at al. 2013). Although there are elements of a conventional teacher-student configuration or even a therapeutic relationship in these cocreativity workshops, the usual intersubjective boundaries between the researcher and participant were effectively redrawn in these extraordinary circumstances. These institutional arrangements remind anybody who needs reminding that, even in this tentative participative reconfiguration, this is an encounter with others who are different. Although the stakes are different for the women residents and the researcher, who can at least head for home after a session, the affective economy created in these workshops although unique for the women, was one that Anja found exhausting. Nonetheless for a couple of hours each week the women were able to exercise some freedom by taking part in an act of making that was designed to enable them to express their needs and preferences. The participative configuration achieved in this project recognized difference but did not treat it as an expression of inequality.

Dialogical Spaces and Equality in Difference

The emergence of cocreative processes such as this have some similarity with a second Asher project that we will discuss because of the insight it may offer for further development of the idea of different but equal, which is central to the cocreative model of participation. In his project *Made in California: NOW* which was part of the Los Angeles County Museum of Art (LACMA) program of exhibitions designed to attract children and their families to the museum, Asher recruited two groups of teenage high school students to reinstall two galleries in the LACMA. Rather than using the traditional authorial vantage point of the curator, this project redraws the intersubjective boundary between production and reception of an exhibition by having the students produce the exhibitions.

The project required each group of teenagers to reinstall one of the standing exhibitions at the LACMA. Asher negotiated a contract between himself, the museum, and the teenagers that required the museum staff not to interfere with the students' production in any way beyond advising them about matters of safety, budget, and conservation. As part of the contract, the students' operational autonomy was to be safeguarded by the presence of an outside facilitator who was to coordinate the reinstallation team and moderate meetings with museum staff. In addition the students were required to use all of the paintings that were currently in the exhibition space, they were not to endanger the safety of the artworks or the audience, and they were not to exceed the budget of five thousand dollars.

Many of the conventional institutional framings of a standing exhibition were not so much subverted as simply ignored by the teenagers. Instead of working with the conventional white cube of gallery space, they painted New York skylines as the backdrop for their exhibition of contemporary American art and lit the pieces with a range of colors and effects. Instead of hanging the most valuable and famous paintings in the prime positions, they tucked them away in corners in favor of more everyday themes such as animal scenes. Instead of hanging pieces against the wall, they commissioned freestanding pedestals on which to place valuable masterpieces. Instead of conventional information panels by the side of each art piece the teenagers offered explanations of why the piece had been chosen and why it had been placed where it was. They also provided a message to visitors explaining their exhibition and hoping that they would enjoy themselves.

As Peltomäki points out, a key feature of Asher's approach was to insist that the teenagers were viewed by the institution as differently placed equals, not just as kids doing their thing. Placed in this curatorial role the teenagers responded in ways that were more dialogical and more redolent of curatorial practices in everyday media spaces than in arts institutions. From an institutional perspective, the exhibition becomes a traditional cultural heritage exhibition (in terms of its content) inflected through the sense-making practices of teenagers, who would not usually participate in this form of culture. In this inflection the visitor is given a strong sense of the cultural values of the teenagers without them becoming the exhibit.

By mandating that the "kids" have independent authority from the outset, Asher did not assume the students' inequality in the museum hierarchy and thus did not seek to rectify any inequality by "educating" the students to make choices informed by the "correct" professional models, and then judging the students according to how well they had absorbed the "proper" museological methods and values. (Peltomäki 2010, 107)

The key point here then, is that equality is not about raising the students up to the level of the professionals, nor is it about reducing the professionals down to the level of the students. Both of these ideas presume a hierarchical conception of inequality rather than a conception of difference, which tends to presuppose that equality is about leveling up, leveling down, or reducing to a lowest common denominator. By contrast, equality for Asher, Peltomäki, and Rancière presupposes difference as its starting point but as a difference of equals. In terms of producing a dialogical space, Asher and Blythe, along with Thieme in the Spheres project see equality as the starting point and difference as the means, rather than inequality being the starting point and homogeneity being the endpoint.

Asher's multilayered installations raise issues about the institutional framing of participation and participants' sense making, especially about individual and collective identity in participatory projects, which would also be usefully considered in the context of participation in digital media. In general, his project of creating conditions for participation in art activities is sensitive to individual experience as well as social relations. People are not employed as tools or types or even as performers to meet his artistic objectives. Instead, by employing people because of their existing expertise, experience, and activity, contractually recognizing the importance of their roles in the project and enabling them to use their experience and perform their activity in a new frame, Asher aligns their experience and status with his artistic situations. By aligning his participants' expertise and experience with his artistic situations, he brings a number of voices into a dialogue, including his own, through which individuated and collective identity as participants in that particular situation is negotiated.

Peltomäki (2010) describes Asher's participative situations as follows:

Instead of engaging in a collective, anonymous experience in the manner of museum or gallery visitors, Asher's participants contribute their names, demeanor, and professional reputations to the artist's work when they agree to be involved. Such professional commitment means that all labor within his work remains individuated for the participants. (115–116)

Making Dialogical Space by Making Participation Sensible

The projects in this chapter experiment with ways of making participation sensible in order to realize the creative potential of dialogical encounters with difference. For Bakhtin (1986), any other (e.g., person or culture) has potential that they cannot see. It is only by coming into dialogue with another who is different from them that this potential can be revealed. One reading of the various projects that we have discussed in this chapter is that they strive, in their different ways, to make participation sensible in order to enable participants to come into dialogue with the other. This language is necessarily abstract to hold the parts of our projects together but it risks rendering participatory projects, sensibility, and dialogue as neat, detached processes. Yet, in the lived experience of particular projects, making participation sensible—setting up a public musical performance that depends on collaboration from strangers, negotiating a professional role for teenagers in a museum that could enhance or damage expensive exhibits and the professional reputation of the gallery—is often dissensual as well as challenging, practically, professionally, and emotionally. So is engaging in dialogue with total strangers.

These projects, all of which are geared toward changing something about conventional ways of being and relating, create situations that can evoke strong feelings that can range from anxiety and vulnerability to hope and pleasure. We have already introduced Sara Ahmed's conceptualization of such situations as affective economies, in which emotions work in concrete ways to mediate relationships between individuals and between individual and collective (Ahmed 2004). In participatory projects, emotions register the proximity of others and otherness, for example, the vulnerability and hope that Humanaquarium performers feel in front of an audience. They also register the strangeness or difference of bodies and space, such as when a dividing wall in a gallery goes missing or when paintings are stacked in the middle of the floor in a museum. In the Spheres project, we also see how emotions align bodily space with social and institutional space and, as

Ahmed has put it, play a crucial role in "surfacing" individual and collective bodies and identities.

In public staged events, such as Humanaquarium and MP3q, teams with strong backgrounds in music draw on the open work tradition in the arts to make a space for dialogue and the creative potential that goes with it. It is possible to read these projects as expressions of the aesthetic and ideological values that inform open work or as playful experiments with the conditions and dynamics of participatory performance and participative experience. We have already seen that Humanaquarium is inspired by a commitment to the idea that audience members have a responsibility to participate and by experimenting with forms of participation to enhance engagement and aesthetic experience. Both the experiments and the values behind them are relevant to understanding the potential for creating dialogical spaces. In practice, the Humanaquarium team's concern to look after participants and, at the same time, to ensure a good performance for the audience brings about an anxious situation for them and probably also for some participants. They encounter each other as interdependent strangers who are intimately visible and sensible to each other. Each can see and respond to the potential and the vulnerability in the other and in the interaction between them. For both, the meaning of the participative experience emerges in and through this encounter and performance.

Asher's projects present a different approach to making participation sensible, based on respect for the professional context of daily work routines rather than creating spectacle or performance. His approach involves contracted participation that recognizes the value of participants' labor and the individuation of their experience. He ensures that participants' professional equality is guaranteed from the outset and that participants are compensated for their labor. Asher aligns participants' usual institutional positions with his materials and installations. Peltomäki argues that in many of his projects, this involves reframing the affective economy of the spaces in which art professionals work, thereby making their feelings about their and other people's professional roles sensible to them. For example, some visitors to the Copley Gallery were unsettled and embarrassed by confronting the gallery owner, their conventional means of managing this relationship having been removed with the need for negotiating a new way of relating sensible to all.

To appreciate the creative potential of Asher's situations and the potential of his work for participatory projects in HCI, a brief overview of the themes that articulate his approach might be helpful. We have already seen the emphasis he placed on formal recognition of equal professional status for the high school students in LACMA as well as the great scope afforded them to curate and install as they wished, coupled with recognition of the need for a responsible approach to budget and the museum pieces. In other projects, which we have not yet discussed, he paid participants, often artists and students, for their labor as docents or as viewers in art galleries, enabling them to interpret their role and responsibilities as they saw fit. In many of his projects, some or all participants remain in their familiar institutional contexts. For example, in one project, he asked employees of three adjoining museums to share a single parking lot for a week. Asher did not prescribe specific parking slots, arrival times, or style of interaction. Leaving plenty of scope for individual interpretation, he hoped that random encounters in the parking lot would bring about varied social interactions.

Asher's projects perturb institutional norms and habitual ways of feeling in the organizations in which his participants have an established role to play. Setting his projects in the participants' usual institutional settings ensures that many elements of the participants' activities are already sensible to them. They know far better than Asher about their car parking arrangements, running a gallery, or installing a show. This approach respects the opening equality and creates a symmetrical relationship that would enable the participants and Asher to learn from each other and to make sense of the project in their own ways rather than according to a premeditated artistic agenda. Freed by Asher's project from habitual understandings of and feelings about their roles, participants are also empowered to take ownership and responsibility for their actions. According to Peltomäki, these transformative effects extend to those not directly contracted, for example, museum or gallery visitors, because the experiential labor of spectatorship is foregrounded.

In Asher's projects then, the creative potential is realized by removing institutional constraints that block people from apprehending their right to take part and their potential as producers. In fact, because Asher sees equality as a precondition for participation, his experiments with redrawing the material and institutional intersubjective boundaries between production and reception of art depend on an egalitarian starting point. From there, he believes that people can teach themselves and teach each other about the art and the art institutions as they participate in Asher's projects. Similar to Rancière, Asher believes that participation can be reconfigured by nudging institutions to make a presumption of equality sensible to all.

The Spheres project seems to pick out all the skeptical reactions one could reasonably have to the idealism of equality as a starting assumption, the right to take part as a usual expectation, and the hope to produce as well as consume, and respond to them with painstaking attention to detail in negotiating a way to work with a necessarily restrictive institutional setting. The women participants were patients in a medium-secure unit of a hospital, in which interactions between patients and visitors (including the researcher) had to be carefully organized and closely monitored, and in which tools to be used in the cocreativity workshops and anything that was made in them had to vetted for safety, especially with respect to concerns about patients self-harming. Institutional norms such as these provide quite a challenge to ideas of dialogue, creativity, and making participation sensible. And yet at the heart of this project was a therapeutic intervention that would be facilitated by the artifacts and that would in many ways train the women in mindful awareness through dialogue.

In cocreativity sessions, the researcher worked individually with each woman, but always accompanied by a research staff nurse, and on a number of occasions by another member of staff as well for safety. Staff and researcher also had to wear an alarm system, and all materials and tools had to be counted in and out of the ward. Nonetheless, the women took part in most of the creativity sessions and, with the researcher, used craft tools and techniques to make beads and charms to be used in their personalized artifacts. They also designed the look of some of the artifacts. They shared photos, music, and personal stories with the researcher for inclusion in videos that would be integral to another of the artifacts, as well as making short stop-motion animations with the researcher. The women said that they enjoyed the activities. Members of staff were impressed by the women's interest and engagement with the activities. Both staff and women seemed to appreciate the opportunity for the women to take responsibility and to make things themselves. The women liked to talk to the staff about what they were doing.

All in all, involving this vulnerable group of women, who are generally not in a position to take any initiative themselves, in the cocreation of personalized artifacts facilitated the design, a sense of ownership, and the women's self-esteem. In this participatory project, enquiry benefitted from the researcher slowly building up intimate relationships with the women in which the limits of dialogue and the potential for sensible creativity could become apparent. It also benefitted from gradually negotiating with staff and women what could and would happen in the participatory sessions and working with the women and staff to find ways to work within the constraints of the situation. This involved learning from those in the situation what the potential for interaction in that situation was. It ensured that participants, staff, and researcher learned from each other in ways that could materially influence perceptions of potential futures in this situation.

Restrictions notwithstanding, running cocreativity workshops in this setting appears to have created an affective economy in the center, especially for the women directly involved, which was borne out of a recognition of the value of their ideas and the individuation of their participative experience. In even such extreme institutional contexts, it seems that the very act of engaging the women, and thereby making participation sensible to them and to the staff of the center, led to some reconfiguration of social relations and the creation of some dialogical spaces.

Concern for the other underpins all of the projects in this chapter. At root, all of them involve encounters with strangers, an empathic response to which can produce local knowledge and social imagination. Empathy is neither a feeling of sympathy nor an ability to identify with the other. It is an imaginative response to the other, an essential component of which is self-other differentiation, which moves along with them as they live out their experience, taking their perspective and anticipating where they are going. In the Humanaquarium project, empathy was facilitated by close contact, very close observation and focused attention, and a commitment to understanding the condition of participation as well as its potential. This was all made possible by the team designing from within the performance and so learning with and from the participants. As well as motivating initiation of the Spheres project, empathy was reinforced by working together in the cocreativity workshops. In LACMA, it was facilitated by a commitment to equality and a concern for the welfare of the other. Asher's individuation of the participative for the students by ensuring their equal standing with the professional shifted boundaries in a way that enabled the students to see new ways of taking part. By imagining what was possible for the students and by making it possible for them to see what was possible, too, he enabled them to decide how to respond as already engaged participants. The imagination to create situations in which people could see what was possible and respond in their own way is also a feature of Humanaquarium, though it carried somewhat less weight in an iterative design discourse that opts for incremental movement.

We framed this chapter as being about understanding the other by making participation sensible. In this context, understanding the other includes understanding the people involved in the project, the roles available, the artifacts that mediate participation, and the ideas, including institutional ideas, that frame participation. The participatory projects in this chapter try to understand by learning from and with the other rather than just about the other (Ingold 2013; Belenky et al. 1997). As participatory projects, they are hoping that by making together, they will learn with and from each other to explore potential and to transform participative experience. In all of these projects, the experience of making together created new participant subjectivities and opened up the technological imaginary. In some of the projects, the learning involved individuation of participative experience. However, in only a few of them was the voice of individual participants in play. By contrast, in the next chapter, we address projects in which the voice, name, and identity of the other are deeply implicated in the ways in which researchers and participants learn with and from each other.

4 Building Personal Relationships

Although there is evidence of individuation of participative experience in some of the projects discussed in chapter 3, it was generally at the level of particular groups. Humanaquarium participants were people attending exhibitions, festivals, and maker faires (Taylor et al. 2011a, 2011b), and the people participating in Asher's installations were students from a particular high school and people who worked in specific galleries and museums, though Peltomäki tells us that they contributed their names. Each project might, by the way, be able to name some participants, but that was not the point of those projects. From the designer or artist's perspective, the projects were relatively impersonal experiments about the potential for and dynamics of collective participation or the sociality of individual participative aesthetic experience. By contrast, the approach to participation in this chapter is personal and durational. We will get to know the names of participants in this chapter because the projects that we will discuss could not have been achieved without researchers and participants getting to know each other. Developing relationships takes time as participants engage in the extended enquiry required to design, deploy, and understand an intervention in a particular context. In some cases, researchers and designers continue to bump into or even call on the people who participated in their projects well after the end of the project. The durational quality of relationships in the projects in this chapter defines them as a distinct genre of participation that is resonant with Suchman's (2007) imaginary of the human in HCI as unfolding biography of culturally and materially specific experiences, relations, and possibilities inflected by each encounter.

The relationships underpinning the projects in this chapter tend to be collaborative in the sense that participants have a voice and authorship of project outcomes is shared (Beech 2008). Configuring participation is an ongoing process in these projects, not the aim or the end that it represented in staged performances. Openness also takes on a different meaning in these projects. As well as open work and work in movement, the openness of social relationships, assembled in the process of reconfiguring participation, is also salient. Perhaps more than in the last chapter, there is also an explicit focus on making a lasting change to interpersonal relationships.

Participants and researchers in these personal projects work together on making sense of the project and its outcomes. They develop meaningful interpersonal relationships through the projects. Bishop's description of the Collective Actions Group (CAG) approach to participative art as "the construction of a collective artistic space amongst mutually trusting colleagues" (Bishop 2011, 1) resonates with the ethics and aesthetics of this genre of participative project. However, in CAG, the artists already trusted and worked with each other when projects started. In some of the projects in this chapter researchers worked with participants who were unlike themselves and initially unknown to them, and mutual trust had to be established during the projects. Therefore, a focus of enquiry in this chapter will be on how creative spaces among mutually trusting participants are made.

A Qualitative Constellation of Possibilities

Understanding how creative spaces with mutually trusting participants are made requires us to understand how people develop a sense of themselves as participants. Dave Beech argues in his essay *Include Me Out!* that participant subjectivity—people's sense of themselves as participants, how they think and feel about it, what they desire in participating, and how their sense of self can be embodied in their voice as participant—is formed in the specific invitation to take part, their response to it, and the social relations that ensue. Given the variety of ways in which these simple social practices unfold in daily life, the binary logic of participation or exclusion cannot generate an understanding of the social context of participation rich enough to accommodate the variety of relations that develop. Similarly, simple binary logics of performer and audience, active and passive, and designer and user are too limited to accommodate the variety of positions available in participatory projects. Beech argues instead for a qualitative approach to understanding participation that accommodates a constellation of possibilities:

If participation entails its own forms of limitations on the participant then the simple binary needs to be replaced with a constellation of overlapping economies of agency, control, self-determination and power. Within such a constellation participants take their place alongside the viewer, observer, spectator, consumer and the whole panoply of culture's modes of subjectivity and their social relations. (Beech 2008, 3)

Beech's qualitative economies of agency, control, self-determination, and power in participatory projects not only challenges binary logics of participation but also the kinds of hierarchical logics commonly used in evaluating civic participation, as well as participatory art and HCI. These hierarchical models assume that participation can be measured on a continuum from full participation to nonparticipation (Arnstein 1969). Arnstein's ladder of participation, at the top of which is citizen control, was developed to give an indication of public participation in policy decision making, especially in urban planning in the United States. Useful though it may have been in that context, for example, by demonstrating the willingness or otherwise of politicians to involve citizens in decision making, it is of limited use in evaluating participatory projects and clarifying the participant's experience of his or her involvement in a project. The issue here is not about having a say in answering a relatively well-defined question; rather, it is about creating space for people with all kinds of experience and expertise to bring their experience to bear on achieving the goal of the project. As Beech's qualitative approach suggests, that is likely to result in a complex constellation of voices and a complex participative experience, in which some participants will have a lot to say at one point in a project and little at other points, some participants take part emotionally or intellectually and others make their voices heard through physical activity and gesture, some participate playfully and others take a goal-oriented perspective. In this context, different participants' enactments of agency and self-determination in lasting relationships may hardly even be commensurable. Agency and self-determination may be expressed in complementary or contradictory, consensual, or dissensual ways. Unlike the one-dimensional situation for which Arnstein's ladder was developed, an accounting of the parameters for action set by and the space made available by participation in these projects is unpredictable and can involve people collaboratively creating new space and new activities in their dialogue.

Making Creative Space for Personhood in Dialogue

In previous chapters we referred to participant subjectivity emerging from the ways in which people position themselves with respect to each other in dialogue. In chapter 1, we argued that in mutually responsive relationships—dialogical relationships—participants treat each other as differently placed centers of value. In chapter 3, we focused on what Rancière's philosophy adds to the mainly Bakhtinian view of dialogue that we have been working with. Our reading of Rancière has expanded the notion of dialogical relationships that we work with when exploring participatory projects. Rancière's work suggests an assumption of equality in diversity as a precondition for dialogical relationships. Without this assumption, even the most benign attempts to create equality involve some participants constantly catching up with others on a trajectory that may not suit their personal qualities. Rancière's work also draws attention to the importance of empathy and mutual learning in dialogue, both of which are based on openness to the creativity of the other. In chapter 3, we used Rancière's ideas about the distribution of the sensible to understand how participation could be reconfigured and new affective economies created. This introduction to dialogical relationships needs some unpacking at this stage if it is to provide the conceptual resources to understand how creative spaces among mutually trusting participants are created and to see the potential of lasting relationships in participatory projects.

A defining characteristic of dialogue and an area of some potential in terms of people collaboratively creating new imaginaries and new activities is the creative tension dialogue enacts between fusing into a single voice and a single identity on the one hand and maintaining dissensus and differentiation of perspectives and voices on the other. According to Bakhtin (1984), for dialogue to happen, participants need to blend perspectives into a conversational unity while simultaneously maintaining the particularity of their own position and voice. For Bakhtin this is the essence of an empathic engagement with the other. Empathy is not about simply becoming the other. If it were, creative surplus would be lost. Dialogue exploits the fact that no two people live the same life and therefore no two people have exactly the same perspective on or expertise in any particular area. By bringing these different experiences and perspectives together to participate collaboratively in a project, it may be possible to forge new imaginaries that neither side alone could have achieved. But this possibility is lost if parties abandon their own perspectives and individual voices.

It is the presence of another person's voice that brings their particular perspective and experience into dialogue. In a piece that prefigures some of Rancière's ideas, Seyla Benhabib (1992) argues that when we relate to each other as concrete others, we view each other as individuals with a particular history, identity, and affective-emotional sensibility. Instead of focusing on what we have in common (which is what we do in generalized abstract relationships), we focus on the differences that exist between us and try to understand from that position of difference the other's needs, desires, and motivation. Our relationships are marked by assumptions of equity and reciprocity, in which each person is entitled to expect the other to recognize them and confirm them as concrete individuals with specific needs, talents, and ability. According to Benhabib (1992), it is through the voice of the other that we come to know them as concrete others with particular identities and sensibilities. It is in how people intone their experience that we begin to see their uniqueness.

Neither the concreteness nor the otherness of the "concrete other" can be known in the absence of the *voice* of the other. The viewpoint of the concrete other emerges as a distinct one only as a result of self-definition. It is the other who makes us aware both of her concreteness and her otherness. (Benhabib 1992, 168)

The Personhood Project

In the Personhood project, the potential for new ways of thinking about and designing for people living with dementia was enhanced by the presence of the particular voice and experiences of these people in design dialogue. We mentioned the Personhood project in chapter 1, in which Jayne Wallace, a jewelry maker, worked with Gillian, who then had mild dementia, and her husband and caregiver John. Jayne met the couple while helping at Alzheimer's day care centers in the northeast of England. The aim of the project was to design digital jewelry to support personal and family experiences that would sustain Gillian's sense of self and personhood even as her memory and cognitive capacity declined. In general, one of the characteristic features of Jayne's work is the close relationship she builds up with participants, based on an empathic engagement over a period of time in which she and the participants learn from each other. Her designs are responses in an ongoing dialogue with her participants, her voice engaging with theirs as they explore particular experiences, such as the experience of living with dementia and the potential for creativity in empathic design dialogue.

Gillian's and John's voices were pivotal in the Personhood project. The project was not about designing for dementia as a cognitive deficit or as a type of experience but for Gillian's, John's, and their family's and friends' experiences of living with dementia. In the reconfiguration of participation that takes place in this project, theirs are the voices and experiences that are made sensible, heard, talked about, and responded to. Jayne developed her cocreative process to ensure that the participants' voices are always present in a way that keeps their experience alive in the project.

Jayne made carefully crafted design probes that responded to her early impressions of Gillian and John. She wanted the probes to involve activities that would be meaningful for them and to be valuable things for their close friends and family, too. She also wanted the probes to facilitate a gentle, reciprocal enquiry that would help develop a mutually trustful relation-ship between her and Gillian and John. A good deal of time was put into designing probes that asked interesting questions in creative ways and that enabled Gillian and John to respond in their own creative ways, too. The probes were designed to enable them to select a way of responding that was comfortable for them or that challenged them a little, whichever they pre-ferred. Jayne then designed pieces of jewelry for them that responded to the sense she had developed of them and their experiences, as well as reflecting her own interests and sensibilities as an artist.

Gillian and John showed particular interest in one probe, the *Self Tree*. This was a series of oval locket-like forms hanging from a small branch. One oval form had the silhouetted image of a woman (representing Gillian) on the front and instructions on the back reading *Please use these objects to tell me about some of the people who make you who you are (family, friends, even people who you've never met, but who have had a real influence on you)*. Gil-lian and John could write or draw their responses on the other seven oval objects, each of which had paper on the front and a fold-out concertina of paper on the reverse. Gillian and John described Gillian's closest relation-ships with family and friends throughout her life. They described the story of each relationship and completed each response with a quote from that person about Gillian.

Gillian and John reported that they felt very comfortable working with the *Self Tree* and that in doing so they had come up with lots of rich memo-ries that were very important to them. When they talked to Jayne about it, John said how amazed he was at how many memories, including the exact words used by people years earlier, Gillian had come up with. He said that most of what was written on the *Self Tree* came from Gillian. Other family members described the importance of their individual relationships with Gillian. Working with the probe seemed to offer everybody involved valuable insights into their lives and also paved the way for further engage-ment with the project. For example, at one point in a conversation about the probes, Gillian described how the process of remembering was very challenging for her. She described it as a door opening a fraction to begin with, that she then tries to push open further. When she was able to open it wider, after great effort, memories seemed to flow back to her in a way that felt like water flooding over her. Listening to Gillian's rich description of the physicality of remembering for her opened up for the research team new perspectives on remembering. Participation in the process enabled varieties of remembering and relating to become sensible, salient, and at times poignant, particularized as they were in Gillian's and John's experiences and stories.

A family learning to live with the experience of dementia has to work hard to make sense of all that is happening to them and all that they are doing. Well-worn phrases that had been the stock-in-trade of ritual communication in the family become unsettled by unexpected responses—no memory of what they meant, no recognition of the person saying them. Against this background, the potential of the digital jewelry that was designed in this project to become the catalyst for new rituals, new interactions, and new meanings has the potential to emancipate those involved from the destabilizing effects of dementia on social relationships. Through interacting with each other around a locket, retelling the stories behind the images, reenacting the experiences, re-creating by adding new content, the drive of experience to expression puts shape on new hard-won meanings to be shared by the family.

Dialogue in a Community of Sense

The Personhood project is a very particular, very personal encounter in which a designer creates probes and jewelry for two people who are learning to live with dementia. It is about Gillian's and John's lives and how empathic design might contribute to sustaining the richness of their relationship, and Gillian's personhood, as they undergo the experience of living with dementia.

We have positioned participatory projects as research projects in HCI. Although this may move outside Jayne Wallace's intentions for the Personhood project, we are interested in developing concepts and frameworks from reading these projects that enable us and HCI to stretch beyond them. This is in part to find connections between projects. It is also to explore the possibility of some limited contextual generalization from specific projects. It is mainly to develop conceptual tools and methods to help us think about participation in HCI. Combining Rancière's distribution of the sensible with Bakhtin's dialogic enables us to use the Personhood project as a scratching post for some concerns we have about design approaches to lived experience, including the lived experience of dementia, beyond this particular project. Used in this way, the Personhood project becomes a site of dissensus on the particular openness of taking part in and learning about lived experience that asks about precisely how the sensible is distributed in participatory design projects and dialogue.

Specifically, Rancière's work encourages us to ask how roles and modes of participation are configured in research and design, and how those roles and modes are influenced by the modes of perception that are supported. In participatory projects, as in other social settings, the accepted distribution of the sensible specifies what is visible and invisible, sayable and not sayable, thinkable and not thinkable. In terms of research projects, it is worth considering whether the sense of prosaic lived experience gets an airing and, if it does, how it is positioned with respect to the sense of institutional or political meaning making. For example, does it recognize the contingent configuration of these two senses, the ways in which they interact to partition the sensible? As Rancière suggests, a material partition of the sensible is also a symbolic partition. Placing some things out of bounds or behind a wall makes a statement about their ownership as well as their visibility and therefore about the inequalities entailed in that mode of perception and organization.

Rancière's idea of a *community of sense* enables us to imagine some wider ramifications of the very personal, bespoke Personhood project. For Rancière (2009b), a *community of sense* is "a certain cutting out of space and time that binds together practices, forms of visibility, and patterns of intelligibility." It is a particular "partition of the sensible" (31). If we use this idea to extrapolate from the partition of the sensible in the Personhood project, we might ask what was made visible, audible, and intelligible in this project in particular, and what aspects of the lived experience of dementia care is made sensible in other communities. We might also ask about the configurations of space and time in these various communities and in their experiences of dementia that binds practice, visibility, and intelligibility in different ways. We might also ask whether design could bring about new communities of sense, as Rancière imagines art and fiction doing when he claims that "fiction invents new communities of sense: that is to say, new trajectories between what can be seen, what can be said, and what can be done" (Rancière 2009b, 49).

In the Personhood project, Gillian's and John's collaborative exploration of their past and present and design of parts of their future was made sensible. Seeing Gillian create something that linked her past and future and that encouraged her to reflect on her present and future relationships made sensible personhood in dementia. Seeing Gillian and John work together on the design probes made visible a creativity that is not generally associated with dementia. There is a cutting out of space and time that works in Gillian's and John's experience of living together and perhaps in the experiences of other families living with dementia. This is where the art of living begins to involve designing new ways of being together, new configurations of visibility, practice, and intelligibility, as practices of remembering and recognizing begin visibly and audibly to change. In the Personhood project, the design potential of bespoke probes and artifacts was highlighted.

In other situations, everyday design might involve a novel use of photographs, a toy, or music. When the person with dementia starts to doubt what happened in the last five minutes and to recognize a husband as an older uncle, accommodations are made in social practices (loved ones may go with the flow) and the trajectory from practice to intelligibility becomes mediated by a kindly pretending for the sake of meaningful connection. In part, this may involve disrupting patterns by introducing homemade interventions—walks, topics, everyday artifacts—around which the person with dementia and his or her caregiver can begin a different dialogue. This configuration is also often characterized by searching for the creativity and personhood that persists no matter what cognitive changes become apparent.

For anybody who has lived or worked with people with dementia and their caregivers, it will be clear that Gillian was in the early stages of dementia when rich interaction is still possible and sensitive designs still make a difference. Although it should be noted that the Personhood project was about Gillian's and John's lives, not about designing for dementia in terms of developing conceptual resources, it may be worth considering other trajectories in dementia care. John McCarthy has two PhD students researching the potential for participation in design of support for people living with dementia and their caregivers. Both are working with people whose dementia has progressed much further than Gillian's had at the time of the Personhood project, developing personal relationships with them and considering with them what resources would enrich their experience. One is working with a small number of people who live in residential care. There, the dialogues that occur between residents and between residents and the PhD student are typically staged in their difference. Whereas Rancière was concerned about making sensible the differences between ordinary discourses that do not obey the same rules or come from the same code, these differences are on the surface in the dialogues that take place in this residential setting. For the other student, who is working with people with dementia and their caregivers in their own homes, discursive differences can become visible in more subtle ways, for example, in the ways in which participants talk about family or privacy, in the childlike ways they talk about pets, or in their repetitions and confusions. Interestingly, wanting to keep secret the practices that reveal dementia is another pattern in this study. In these projects, the practices, forms of visibility, and patterns of intelligibility that are available bring about a quite different community of sense to the one in the Personhood project. It is often a dissensual and discordant community of sense in which participative experience and subjectivity is continually in flux.

Configuration of the sensible can be quite different again for research teams, community caregivers, and advocates. In these contexts, engagement can be at a distance in time and space, occasionally visiting to chat and observe, and analyzing at a distance. The challenge here is to develop a cutting out of space and time that keeps the experience of living with dementia alive in the chatting, observation, design response, and writing. The presence of the particular voice—including using whatever creative means can be conjured up to keep it present in the research—is key. The richest recordings, transcripts, or field notes may enable even those not present at the time to hear Gillian tell her particular story in which the physicality of remembering is made visible. An imaginative, empathic response suggests a cutting out of space and time that considers remembering to be an embodied, sensory searching for coherence and perspective. That gives everybody involved a lot more to work with than a general expectation of memory lost. Keeping it alive nudges participatory relationships toward a cutting out of space and time that aligns with Gillian's and John's experience, not with an abstracted notion of living with dementia.

When researchers ultimately leave to go back to speak to their colleagues in labs, studios, and at conferences, what do they take with them? Following Rancière, we might want to suggest a sense of unease about the assumed inequality that develops as dementia progresses and concern about the partition of the sensible around the experiences we are interested in. Unease, concern, feeling a bit disturbed might also help keep the experience of living with dementia alive. In our limited experience in this area, this takes two different paths. In one, the design project becomes for researchers a site in which preconceptions about designing for dementia care become perturbed. For us, assistive technology, the label, and the design practice became problematic, suggesting as it did excess dependency that we were not sure we would want to visit on our loved ones. For example, the potential intrusiveness of GPS unwittingly worn by a person going for a walk (wandering or walking) or sensors in a home distributing potentially private information became ethical and political. This does not imply a naive rejection of such supports. We can both easily think of situations in which they could be invaluable. Rather, it insists on an empathic ethical enquiry in each particular case into the politics of using these technologies. The presence of a particularly intoned voice makes the distribution of the sensible political, a contested area, and a questioning of the distribution of the sensible becomes integral to determining the value(s) of these technologies especially their participatory values.

In a second path, the design focus shifts to community, for example, to the need for dementia-friendly communities. On this path, researching in a participative way the experience of dementia and dementia care leads one to see the change, and therefore the design, that matters in community. If communities were better prepared to see the world in the way in which a person with dementia may, would the person with dementia have to have GPS support or nursing home care as early as some do? One of the PhD students previously mentioned, who works in this area, has remarked on her growing sense of becoming part of an in-group—or a public—who see themselves as on the side of people with dementia and their caregivers. They worry about the invisibility of everyday dementia experience, the taboo around talking about dementia, and they try to make dementia intelligible to the wider community so as to make the experience of living with it more manageable for people living with dementia. This student runs a number of social media sites for caregivers, families, and others involved in or concerned about dementia to share experiences and to support each other. In her work, an inclusive approach tries to make sensible the creativity and pleasure that is largely absent from discourses on dementia and dementia care. Finding where the creativity and personhood is and making it visible may suggest intelligibility that had not been available before. It may also make sensible the differences in discourses about the experience of dementia and dementia care, which can be moved to one side in favor of a concerted effort or a united advocacy.

In our discussion of the Personhood project and our extensions beyond the specific project to a broader focus of the communities of sense that spring up around the experience of dementia, we have been keen to highlight the creativity and personhood of participants: Gillian and John in their lives, other people living with dementia, caregivers, advocates, and researchers. To some extent, we have used the Personhood project as a jumping off point to talk about the potential of a dialogical approach to participation to focus attention on the power of the voice of the other to make us aware of particular experience and individuality. Given the focus on dementia, something that most of us struggle to comprehend and imagine, this discussion inevitably veers toward trying to understand elusive creativity in the ways in which people live with this difficult-to-imagine condition.

In the next section, we explore another elusive creativity, in this case the skilled practice of VJs (video jockeys). We focus on the potential of a dialogical approach to understanding and supporting skilled practice in the context of a project in which the researcher develops a community of VJs, whose practices create a community of sense that the researcher is keen to redistribute.

Understanding from within Dialogically Structured Relations with VJs

Skilled practice is generally thought of as embodied and tacit. Therefore, the idea that skilled practice be understood by talking about it is quite complicated. Though practitioners may be great at articulating their practice, telling stories about it, exploring what it feels like, and so on, they are less good at specifying the action (see Ingold 2013 for a discussion of this distinction). In this section, we discuss a participatory project in which an HCI researcher, who has some skill in the area being researched and is therefore not entirely an outsider, tries to understand the skilled practice better to support its performance with interactive technology. His skill in the area enabled easier access to dialogically structured relations with his participants, from within which he could explore the potential of their practice and performance as an insider with credibility in the dialogue, yet remaining different when it came to highly skilled, publicly performed, expressive practice.

John Shotter (2000) claims that the aim of participatory research is to help "participants attend to the spontaneous, dialogical involvements in which they originate and sustain their practice" (130) so that, by being able to see them, participants are also able to see the beginning of new practices. We paired this with Wittgenstein's (1953, 61) discussion of understanding as knowing how to go on. We see each of the projects in this chapter as enquiries into dialogical involvements, understanding of which enables participants to go on. Enquiring into dialogical involvements to see in a way that enables new practices to develop is central and explicit in the aims and methodology of the VJs project (Hook et al. 2013).

The VJs project involved designing interactive technologies to support and enhance the practice and experience of live VJ performances. VJs are live performers whose practice involves the manipulation and presentation of visual media, such as video clips or computer-generated imagery, to audiences in settings ranging from nightclubs to art galleries. The project was supported by ongoing relationships that Jon Hook, the lead researcher and designer in the project, had developed with four practicing VJs and VJ collectives, consisting of seven VJs in all. Jon also had a strong involvement in the live performance scene and was able to engage with the VJs as a fellow traveler, as someone who understood enough of the partition of the sensible in that community to be able to see the challenges and the potential. Although it is clear that Jon initiated the project and the invitations, the project reports describe a mutuality of involvement and mutual learning. It seems that the VJs were as keen to understand and design for their evolving practice as the researchers were and, responsive to that keenness, the project was set up to hear their strong voices in the design and development of the next generation of technologies they are likely to use.

The research challenge was to identify the what and how of VJ practice in order to design interfaces for VJs that would enable them to use digital technology to perform in a manner that would make live experiences available to their audiences. One of our interests in the project is in the creative trusting space that Jon constructed in his conversations with the VJs to help them and him see the "dialogical involvements in which they originate and sustain their practice" (Shotter 2000, 130) and the beginning of new practices that enables them to go on in their evolving performances. As well as already having a working relationship with them, as researcher and designer he managed the creative tension between fusion and differentiation by keeping a tight focus on the individual and quite different performances as the basis for making tacit practice sensible and open for discussion.

In the first of two studies, Jon and a professional filmmaker followed the VJs as they prepared, practiced, and performed their work during a month-long audiovisual arts festival and made a documentary film about them, called *A Short Film about VJs*. The documentary was structured as a response to engagement with each of the VJ's practices and performances. For example, Hook et al. (2011) describe the overall style of the video as follows:

A montage style was adopted where interview footage, shot throughout the filmmaking process, was placed alongside relevant scenes of the subject at work or in performance. This approach was chosen to create a film that portrayed our interpretation of the performer as a reality or truth that was depicted with their words and actions alone. As a consequence we hoped to evoke a much stronger response than if we had actively spoken our ideas with the addition of a narration track. (1267)

They also describe their particular response to each VJ's practice. For example, their vignette of Tron Lennon, a collaboration between two electro-acoustic musicians, involves mirroring back to them the individuality of their performances with a view to enquiring into their particular approach to collaborative practice.

The vignette emphasises the contrast between the practices of John and Paul. We hope to show that rather than co-creators of a single practice they are two performers, with well-defined practices of their own, in collaboration. Interview footage of Paul speaking almost exclusively about his desire for finite control and powerful manipulation of video content is set next to John's discussion of the adaptation and misappropriation of technology. Footage of Paul and John's visuals are shown in isolation to illustrate the contrasting aesthetics that are combined to produce the final visual output. We hope through the isolation and juxtaposition of aspects of both practices to enquire about the reasoning for, and consequences of, their collaboration. (Hook et al. 2011, 1268)

Because it captures subtle details of practice and performance, the film illustrated an initial research response to the work and invited the VJs to take the position of viewer of their own performances. As well as supporting ethnography of the work, the film also became a focus in the ongoing dialogue between Jon and the VJs about their practice. This dialogue took two forms. The first was a focus group combined with individual interviews, in which the four VJs or VJ collectives got the opportunity to discuss and reflect on their own practice and on each other's. A number of VJs talked about wanting to evoke particular experiences in their audiences. Andrew had designed 3D visuals in his performance to stir up feelings of astonishment or amazement, and Toby spoke about a performance called Privy, a "kind of dream like thing where if you sit back and let it wash over you it is a very emotional experience." Paul referred in conversation to the way in which he intentionally disrupts narrative flow in his performance: "a lot of the stuff I'm actively trying to do is actually trying to fracture narrative as well, and that's where the needle dropping thing comes from." VJing is a visible performance and the VJs did not want technology that would make their actions invisible to the audience. They were also keen to retain qualities of improvisation and responsiveness in their performances. For example, Elliot talked about the centrality of feedback in live performance as follows, "before we couldn't do this live feedback, the event back into itself that we can do now, and that puts VJs centre stage and gives them a reason to be there."

The second conversation was a creative response in which each of the VJs made a short reedit of the documentary film to emphasize their individual response to a particular issue in the film or that came up in the focus group. The creative response is again presented by the creator(s) to the other participants. Tron Lennon, a pair of VJs who work together, created a response in which

short sounds play and loop in tandem with video clips of both John and Paul manipulating their instruments and controllers. At points the sound stops and footage of the pair speaking about the turntable as a tactile controller is shown. At one point visuals are scrubbed through in time with a video of Paul's hand scratching a record. The response concludes with a clip of a man speaking about the unison between the sound of his speech and the moving image, throughout which the audio is out of sync. (Hook et al 2011, 1272)

In presenting this response Paul emphasized the importance of tactility in their performance. Cutting simple movements and fades into the film of him interacting with his equipment was meant to illustrate his desire for a mapping between physical gesture and video.

Aspects of the conversations between VJs suggest an emerging community of sense that values the visibility and intelligibility of live performance. The VJs want space organized in a way that would enable the audience to make sense of their performance based on the visibility of expressive interactions and visual display outcomes. Although it is central to their practice that technology be present, they do not want it to intrude but instead to emphasize the sensory immediacy of their performance as it aligns with audience experience.

Jon responded to the conversations by designing for the VJs' future practices, performances, and experiences. He did this by means of an extended idiographic engagement with one of the VJs, Andrew. The idiographic approach was adopted to facilitate close participation of the designer and the VJ in an enduring relationship in which they could respond spontaneously and openly from within a collaborative working relationship as they experienced performance and design together. In the moment-to-moment responsivity of this relationship, both participants are able to respond to transitory understandings of where they have gotten to so far and in anticipation of where they are next likely to go or how they should go on from where they are (Shotter 2008). As they do so, their participatory practice is organized from within their activity together and therefore has the living quality of a felt and valued responsive engagement rather than something distant and formulaic. In terms of the creative space, in the VJs project, it is a living, dynamic, spontaneous space in which the transitory and contingent nature of understanding, the responsiveness of action, and the felt quality of participation are encouraged.

The focus of this chapter is on personal relationships in participation that involve a history of relational encounters in which people get to know each other's stories, hopes, and voices, and in which design projects are geared toward making those voices sensible. Though the Personhood and VJs projects differ in some respects—the former being about designing for something that people are undergoing and learning to live with and the latter designing for skilled practice, the former involving design in response to participative experience and the latter designing with participants and within the experience—they are nonetheless clear examples of work in this participatory genre. However, personal relationships do not have to be as individual as they were in those two projects, in which it is easy to imagine friendships developing after the projects have finished. Participatory projects in larger organizational contexts can also be personal when participants step out of their ascribed organizational roles and encounter each other as self-defined concrete others with distinctive voices. We see an example of this in the BOSOP project.

Trust and the Emergence of an Imaginary in BOSOP

BOSOP (Better Outpatients Services for Older People) was a one-year project working with the staff and outpatients of the Royal Hallamshire Hospital in Sheffield, United Kingdom, doing an experience-based redesign of the older people's outpatient services (Bowen, Dearden, Wolstenholme, and Cobb 2011).

There were a number of contextual precursors to the project, appreciation of which may help with understanding the dynamics of relationship building within the project. One was a persistent sense of a struggling National Health Service (NHS). The NHS is the comprehensive general medical service of the United Kingdom. Although discussed in prewar years, it was launched in 1948 with three core principles: that it meet the needs of all, that it be free at the point of delivery, and that it be based on clinical need, not ability to pay. When it was launched it was seen internationally as a remarkable experiment in health care, an outstanding example of socialized medicine, and a hugely ambitious achievement. Although it has generally been highly valued by the public, a troubled history of political stewardship and management has in recent times disenchanted many people (Webster 2002). A rolling program of reform has been experienced by some participants as creeping managerialism and by many as destabilizing. Some staff and patients would have seen the healthcare reform program as an attempt to take away their NHS, something that had been a source of great pride as one of the great public service achievements. Initiatives associated with the reform agenda have to be seen against a background of some ideological opposition to public service, a perceived commitment to managerialism, and a media-led discourse on the wastefulness of the NHS. A significant change from the early phases of the reform agenda, signaled in the NHS Operating Framework for 2006–2007, put patients at the center of reform. It involved a move from "targets-driven" to "incentives-driven" change with the key incentive being responsivity to patient needs (Bate and Robert 2007).

Another contextual factor was the growing influence of design as a discipline in debates about public service in the United Kingdom. At around the time of this project, the British Design Council was producing provocative discussion papers, the RED papers, which argued for a role for design in helping solve what was considered to be the systemic failure of many public services to deliver. One of the media tropes on the public services was their inability to cope with increasingly complex societal demands through what are perceived to be unwieldy, bureaucratic organization structures. Reform was the order of the day and the Design Council RED papers commented on plans for reform from a design perspective (Cottam and Leadbeater 2004). This approach gained some traction in health service reform, leading to the use of experience-based design in some projects (see Bate and Robert 2007 for examples). Its use must have created a difficult participative experience for staff for whom all of this would mean a great deal of organizational change, giving up some of their traditional roles and powers and engaging in a long-term, perspective-changing conversation with patients as the experts on their own needs and their experience of the service.

Against this background of change and uncertainty, BOSOP was a project run by the user-centered healthcare design (UCHD) team, within the larger National Institute for Health Research–funded partnership program entitled Collaboration for Leadership in Applied Health Research and Care in South Yorkshire (CLAHRC-SY). Under this program, the UCHD team comprised NHS staff and university staff, all of whom had their time on the project funded by CLAHRC-SY. The UCHD core team included, from the hospital, the director of professional and allied services and a nurse practitioner who worked as clinical researcher and project manager on BOSOP, and, from the university, the professor of human-centered design (Peter), the professor of interactive systems design, and an industrial design research associate. To this was added a group of older outpatient service users and a group of outpatient staff.

Aware of the need to establish good working relationships among staff, patients, and the core team, the research team designed a process for building commitment to the project and for building mutual trust within it. The process involved a gradual buildup of the team through small incremental events and collaborative activities in which the main objectives were to share experience and come up with plans for improvement. The research team was also keen to emphasize participants' shared ownership of the project.

The project brought together twelve older patients and caregivers, some patient advocates from a voluntary organization, nine hospital staff, and designers. The patients, caregivers, and advocates were recruited from medical outpatient clinics and via Sheffield Churches Council for Community Care, a voluntary organization that provides support in areas such as hospital attendance and discharge. The staff, including two staff nurses, a head nurse (or ward sister in the United Kingdom), two clerical staff, an ambulance dispatcher, and a consultant geriatrician, were recruited by word of mouth in the hospital and through the specific encouragement of their colleagues on the research team. Initially members of the research team met patients and advocates to talk to them, reassure them, and gather stories of their experience. Then two half-day events were held, one for patients and caregivers and one for staff, to share their experiences and stories. At a third event, the two groups shared their stories with each other and used them to agree on the service areas that needed improvement. Participants then formed two codesign teams to discuss those areas and to propose improvements. Finally, a plenary event was organized to review, prioritize, and initiate implementation projects.

The gradual introduction of patients and staff to each other was designed to slowly build up a space in which all participants could trust each other. It would be a mistake to assume that the two groups, patients and staff, were internally coherent and came to the project with mutual trust established. In fact, it turned out that each group contained people with quite different experiences and perspectives, hence, the need for these groups to work independently first to facilitate participants to get used to hearing other staff or patients rehearse their experiences and ideas. Even after that phase, interaction between frustrated patients, unhappy with the hospital service, and frustrated staff, unhappy with the resources that were available to them, could easily have produced little more than a discourse of blame and defense. Indeed the project team notes that participants' understanding of the project and their roles in it as agents of change evolved only gradually throughout the project (Bowen et al. 2011). For example, initially when patients shared their experiences, staff became defensive, identifying resource limitations or logistical demands that bring about difficult situations rather than listening to how it felt for patients. The design team restated the aim of sharing experiences and understanding how the other feels to be a patient or member of staff. Time working on the project and small victories along the way, for example, moments of sharing frustrations, and one of the staff—a health support worker called Tracey—telling patients about their "book of bullshit," the half-truths told to patients who were frustrated by waiting in the hope that any explanation would be better than none, helped build up a level of trust and common ground between staff and patients.

Bringing patients and staff together not only brought a wider range of perspectives and voices together but also put each in a position in which they could hardly fail to see their own discourse from the other's perspective. Take a story told by one of the patients, Ruth, of her anxiety over being late:

We were a little bit late and we couldn't find anywhere to park [...] so [my daughter] went ahead to get my appointment and I fell, right outside the Accident & Emergency place. [...] There was an ambulance driving through. [The driver] stopped and got out and a man that was walking by, they came and lifted me up. They were fantastic. It shook me up. [...] I grazed my elbow and I grazed my hip but I didn't break anything and we got in there and saw the doctor and I was okay. [...] You see I'm frightened of being late. Q2: Ruth, Patient (Bowen et al. 2011, 156)

This made visible something that might have seemed relatively invisible to some staff, the impact of parking space on being late for appointments. The fact that the patient was shaken by the fall and that her emotional response was exacerbated by her fear of being late had an effect on everybody and contributed to parking and road layout being on the agenda for improvement.

Ruth telling her story of the anxiety over being late for an appointment and Tracy telling patients about the "book of bullshit" are examples of the kind of affective economy that is created through the redistribution of the sensible in participatory relationships, which we discussed in chapter 3 (Ahmed 2004). The kind of dialogical encounter that enables parties to see things from the other's perspective without giving up their own position, which we have described elsewhere in this chapter, also played out here in a concrete context.

The experiential and relational dimensions of Tracey's disclosure to patients of the existence and function of the "book of bullshit" are likely to be more precisely analyzed by considering the dialogic involved in disclosing in this particular context. It might help us understand, for instance, why staff had decided in preparation for the event to present this information to patients under the potentially less provocative label of "standard excuses," and why in the moment Tracey revealed the original label and admitted the way staff actually thought of the situation, and why that admission prompted laughter and a release of tension in the room (Bowen et al. 2011). The interpersonal process of managing boundaries and creating new relational spaces and new joint activities in an organizationally difficult and potentially vulnerable context is likely to consist of a number of such moments that can at best be supported by appropriate openness and support in the participatory design process. The creative space is a space in which participants not only have to have an appropriate level of trust in each other but also in a process that enables them to develop trust at a pace that suits them. There is some evidence of that happening in BOSOP, especially in the measured disclosures and their reception.

However, the emergence of elements of mutual trust and creative activity was not always sufficient to retain the commitment of all BOSOP participants. Staff morale dipped during the series of codesign workshops when several staff participants became less involved. One staff member, part of whose role was to schedule appointments and meet outpatients as they arrived, was active in the first joint meetings and was very enthusiastic about some very simple improvements that were trialed (e.g., giving him a laminated map of the building to use with patients). Later he was very reluctant to come to meetings, feeling that his time would be better spent doing his clerical work, concern about which he had raised in the staff experience event. Similarly, a nurse participant, who led one of the codesign groups for several meetings, eventually declared she wouldn't be involved anymore. She was reluctant to share her reasons for this surprising decision, but it eventually transpired that her involvement was resented by her coworkers because they felt that her attendance at these "training sessions" left them with more work to do. Toward the end of the project when the researchers were keen to disseminate their activities to a larger audience of staff, they proposed a lunch event at which they would offer sandwiches and light refreshments in exchange for staff time. Some of the participants were reluctant and one voiced her concerns saying that she found it difficult to attend free lunches when she didn't always have sufficient budget to put soap in the toilets. When seen against government ambivalence about supporting these workers and government cuts in material resources including staffing, concern about colleagues having to pick up one's work is hardly surprising. It does, however, remind us of the influence of the broader organizational and ideological context for projects such as BOSOP.

Creating a space in which people could work together as colleagues on outpatient department redesign was a key factor in the successes that the BOSOP project had. However, on reflection, it is also clear that constructing a creative, mutually trusting space in a context such as BOSOP, with its complex contextual precursors and working relationships outside the project team, is an ongoing process of working out sustainable relationships among the research team, hospital staff, patients, and patient advocates. Participation is not a one-off event; experience-centered participatory design has to become embedded in organizational values and practices, and specific participatory projects always have to be seen with respect to the particular context in which they operate. The plurality of people's experiences in specific contexts ensures that interventions and actions, such as setting up BOSOP, come with a variety of dialogic intonations and resonances to the already uttered and the anticipated, responses to which may be pivotal in researcher's or designers' attempts to construct a creative participative space.

Making Creative Spaces by Attending to Dialogical Personal Relationships

In some of the projects in chapter 3, creative spaces were constructed around open work to explore the dynamics of reconfiguring participation. They were spaces in which people encountered situations that encouraged them to act different than the way they usually would. By contrast, in the current chapter, the challenge for projects and participants has been to construct spaces in which people are taken as they come and enabled to define themselves in the context of the project. This approach to participation is more in keeping with Rancière's idea that reconfiguring social order requires a change in the distribution of the sensible. In the projects reviewed in this chapter, openness and reconfiguration are entwined in interesting ways. When people participate in their own ways, the result is likely to be a dialogical creative space in which interactivity and identity shape each other. Fluid relationships begin to take shape in the lived experience of openness in communication and self-expression. People begin to define themselves as they negotiate those relationships with each other. In BOSOP, patients and staff became concrete, named others with autobiographies and hopes. In the Personhood project, Jayne Wallace had to negotiate a balance among researcher, supporter, and friend that was true to how she saw herself when she was visiting a couple living with dementia. The couple, in their engagement with her, remembered their life together and imagined their future. In the VJ project, VJs began to define themselves as enquiring into the future of their medium and their practice, appreciating its biography, presence, and projected future as they do. This was a creative space that emerged from personal relationships taking shape (reconfiguring) through particular histories of relational encounters during the project.

The dialogical creative space is also a space in which participants self-define as they continuously configure and reconfigure their participation. Benhabib's incisive characterization of relating to each other as concrete others and as viewing and hearing each other as individuals with a particular history, identity, and affective-emotional sensibility is premised on an assumption of self-definition. In a phrase that risks becoming worn from use, self-definition is not a goal in these projects; it is the starting assumption. Interestingly Benhabib's language is quite similar to Suchman's when she talks about engaged participants, who may be people or things, having "an autobiography, a presence, and a projected future" (Suchman 2007, 23).

Following Benhabib, the *voice of the other* is key to the kinds of encounters, relationships, and spaces that we are interested in in this chapter. Voice is a particularly evocative term to which we have returned a number of times in our own work (McCarthy and Wright 2004; Wright and McCarthy 2010). It embraces the affective and individualizing tones that help identify the particularity of a person as an emotional-volitional center of value in dialogue. In dialogue, we sometimes hear other people's voices even before they speak and we listen closely to their tone to get a sense of how they feel. It also embraces the idea of people giving voice to their experience in the stories of events that they tell to others and the ways in which they tell them. The idea of voice also encourages us to ask whose voices are heard and which voices are ignored in participatory projects. In HCI, this may include consideration of the voices articulated in the artifacts with which people interact, the particular autobiographies and orientations that they convey. And in design projects and other projects in which professional status can divide, voice can be used to communicate authority.

Reconfiguring Professional Knowledge

The creative spaces in this chapter are spaces in which relationships are formed and imaginaries are constructed and realized through dialogue. They are dialogical spaces, spaces in which people try on a variety of positions and perspectives—and voices—because of their personal commitment to the project. In these projects, people with different experience, expertise, and interests came together to rethink lived experience, a service, and live performance. In contrast with Bishop's Collective Actions Group for whom the dialogue was among a number of trusted artist colleagues, in the Personhood, BOSOP, and the VJs projects, the creative space had to be constructed from the foundations up. In each case, a number of people, all of whom had a stake in the project and each of whom had different experience and expertise with respect to the project, were invited to take part in dialogue with each other on the assumption of equal but different and valued. Among the people involved in these projects were those who would have been seen by some of the others as being experts and professionals—doctors, staff nurses, designers, artists, and so on. This is likely to be the case in most participatory projects and therefore raises issues that deserve consideration in a framework for participation that includes personal relationships as a genre. Jeremy Till is an architect who has thought about the barriers to participation when expertise and professional status can be seen as creating asymmetrical relationships in terms of their value to the project (Till 2005).

In cultures that highly value professional knowledge, it can be difficult for other, nonprofessional voices to be heard, often resulting in unresponsive discourse. Equally, nonprofessionals can be perceived of as belittling professional knowledge. Till argues that what is needed to make the most of participation between professionals and the public that use their services is an approach that transforms the expectations and futures of both sides by empowering the public to engage without disavowing professional knowledge. He calls this *transformative participation*. He suggests that it involves a change in how professionals (architects in his case) view their expert knowledge and also a change in how that knowledge is enacted in dialogue between professionals and the people who use their services.

Transformative participation creates local knowledge by reconfiguring the sensible in a reimagination of professional knowledge from the perspective of the service user. That is to say, it is reimagined in terms of user experience and in a vernacular language that users understand. This requirement to make sensible is more challenging than simply giving knowledge away. Just making professional knowledge more accountable and transparent changes nothing about the way in which it is framed. As long as it is in the form of technical data and formal representations, any access that users have to it is always on the professional's terms. Professional knowledge presented from the perspective of the professional is remote from the user's experience and needs and protects the professional from having to engage on the user's terms at all. According to Till, a gap between the specialist and the nonspecialist opens up in architecture's specialist pursuit of techniques and aesthetics detached from the everyday world. In architecture, where the gap between the specialist and the nonspecialist is largely rhetorical and perhaps most often used to create a protective barrier for the professionals, using vernacular language is a real option and could be the first step for the professional engaging with the participatory process.

An expert using the vernacular language and curious about the needs and experiences of their nonspecialist participants demonstrates their respect for the everyday knowledge of the user and acknowledges the potential for transformation that would come about by engaging with it as valuable to design. Reinvigoration is apparent when this process becomes an expanded dialogue. As Sanoff, cited in Till, puts it:

the knowledge of the user-expert is necessary to state the obvious and the commonplace in order to expand the narrowness of vision often found in highly trained people. (Sanoff 2000, cited in Till 2005, 34)

Reality bites through encounters with concrete others. The earlier such encounters happen, the earlier the dialogue in participation becomes real, as experts face the contingencies, dependencies, and the messiness of user experience on which realization of their vision depends. This is also true of users confronting the realities against which their dreams and vision are likely to bump. As encounter moves over time into a collaborative relationship, two different ways of seeing the context for design are brought together in dialogue leading to ideas that may otherwise have been unlikely to emerge.

Till's analysis of the challenge that participatory processes pose for experts (architects in his case) redresses a balance by also attending to the expert's participative experience and thereby focusing on the mutuality of participation with all parties having to move to engage. It also acknowledges a fluidity and dialogic in position taking and exchange. For example, Till notes that architects are citizens and users, too. Staff in hospitals may also have been patients or at least know people who have been patients. The designer of expressive interactive systems is also the user of such systems in the very work of developing the interactive systems for the VJs. Users are also likely to be professionals and experts in other contexts, too. In dialogue, each of them has the job of transforming expert knowledge into user knowledge and user knowledge into expert knowledge, and may be able to use their experience of different positions in different contexts to do so.

Till sees the creative space in which these transformations occur as a negotiation space. He recognizes the contested nature of the space when the personal wishes and beliefs of the public and the visions of experts come into contact with each other in participatory encounters. Because the participatory process makes these different values and experiences sensible, it brings forward the moment when the political nature of the space has to be dealt with. However, as Till sees it, participation of users early in the negotiation of this political space opens up new opportunities, framing the process as a "negotiation of hope" (Till 2005). This is a forward-looking approach that contrasts with a conception of design as problem solving, which is inevitably backward looking. Till's sentiment ties very strongly into experience in BOSOP, in which it was hard for all sides to move from looking at problems to looking forward to new ways of doing things. The framing and solving of a problem is an exclusionary act.

The approach to framing imaginaries as negotiation spaces that Till offers is based on Forester's (1985) work. It is the idea that what occurs in participatory dialogue is sense making, not problem solving. Participants together in a creative space use their best judgment in the face of different positions, convictions, feelings, and an underlying sense that the design imagination and the means of going on is always open and ambiguous. Against this background, he sees the space as a conversational space geared toward making best sense rather than forcing a consensus, when best sense acknowledges that there is no single solution and many different perspectives. For Till, "this inevitably leads to the acceptance of difference rather than the imposition of a false equality" (Till 2005, 40).

Patients telling their stories in BOSOP and similar experience-based design projects find their agency precisely in their voice as patient. Trying to turn them into designers or health service specialists would put them in a position in which they are always trying to catch up and always made aware of their limited understanding of design and health services. They speak with authority as patients, with the particular experiences that are different from those of the other stakeholders around the table. It is in their difference that they can find themselves leading and giving direction. In interaction design, the disappearing designer and the designer pretending to be the same as users runs the same risk of replacing dialogically productive distance and space with illusory sameness that compresses the space for exploring and questioning values, practices, and experience.

The projects reviewed in this chapter and the genre of participation that they exemplify encourage us to consider participatory projects from the perspective of their boundaries with respect to what can be seen, heard, thought, and made and who is allowed to do each of these. The idea of a community of sense opened up particular examples of the relational to consideration of the patterns of partition of the sensible, which they exemplify, and how those patterns may correspond to other patterns of partition that develop in communities. Understanding design as a process of configuring participation through a redistribution of the sensible suggests directions and questions for the projects yet to be discussed. These include questions about the thresholds of participation that take us into the area of disidentification and outside belonging in chapter 5 and questions about vernacular language and the nonspecialist public in chapter 6. Both of these chapters describe examples of articulations of space and time that bind together practices, forms of visibility, and patterns of intelligibility.

5 Belonging in Community

In the last chapter, we focused on personal relationships between people working together on participatory projects. In this chapter, our focus is on projects that seek to work with communities. Most people feel that they belong to several communities simultaneously. Some are quite narrow, such as climbing clubs or communities of researchers interested in a specific topic. We turn up to community events, recognize and salute people there, and are in turn recognized by many of those present. We chat with some and do stuff with others. We have a sense of how these events go, the pattern of activity, the boundaries between the informal chatting and the formal activities, who is likely to say and do what and why. Our past history of personal engagement means we have something in common with others, for example, an interest in and knowledge of climbing, shared experiences of climbing trips and knowledge of the adventures and difficulties of those climbs, an appreciation for the skills, and a shared commitment to the values associated with climbing. All of these things create a sense of belonging.

Although narrow in focus, the sense of belonging in research communities and climbing clubs can run very deep. The sense of belonging in other communities, such as those of the towns or neighborhoods we grew up in, can be more diffuse and harder to pin down than clubs and societies, but they also can be deeply felt. Living in and growing up in a particular town can bring with it a deep immersion in the practices of that place and all the implicit understanding that goes with that. Even after being away for a few years, we are able to join in casual conversation as insiders, knowing the topics and the appropriate level of chat that people feel comfortable with. A sense of there being different modes of belonging in community runs through much research on community participation.

Settled Communities

There are many different approaches to community in HCI and community computing. For example, community of practice (Lave and Wenger 1991) is widely used in HCI to analyze social and organizational aspects of experience with technology, and communities of interest supported by social media are well documented (e.g., Ploderer, Wright, Howard, and Thomas 2009). However, in this chapter, our main interest is in participation in community in the sense of people living and being together.

Communities of people living together offer opportunities and challenges for designers who often start as outsiders and have to develop and communicate a beneficial role for design in those communities. Some community computing research approaches these challenges by treating community as theoretically and pragmatically settled and then exploring the added value that technology could bring. For example, as we saw in chapter 2, the Bespoke project aimed to contribute to activist-led projects to revitalize Callon and Fishwick by introducing digital media to help local people tell their own stories and work through problems in the area (Frohlich et al. 2011). The project set up a team of community citizen journalists to report on issues that were important to them and their community (Blum-Ross et al. 2013). In other projects, community networks have been used as online augmentation of existing communities, for example, the Blacksburg Electronic Village project attempted to provide online community resources to a town using a web-based portal. This enabled people in Blacksburg to create pages with the aim of "increased access to information and easier participation in community life" (Carroll and Rosson 1996, 71). Similarly in their RuralConnect Living Lab Project with Wray Village, the University of Lancaster developed a long-term relationship with the village of Wray, starting with installing a wireless mesh network across the entire village. Among other projects they carried out was the installation of a touch screen photo display in the village shop, the use of which researchers monitored over a period of time. As part of the same project, a display notice board was later installed. Research on the use of these devices in Wray highlighted their role in providing an accessible repository for community history and a catalyst for community sharing.

The projects in Wray, Blacksburg, and in Fishwick and Callon start from the assumption that the communities with which the projects are working are already established and have value for the people living in those areas. Studdert (2006) warns against such abstractions of community because they tend to neglect the lived experience of being part of community, "the conjoined actions, speech, and imaginations of the social world itself" (3–4). He sees community being as always multiple, hybrid, and never permanent, brought into being through sociality and impossible to perform without others present. For him, it is precisely in the experiences of getting on together and imagining together that community is made sensible.

Bauman (2001), in his essay on community, contrasts the sense of danger and insecurity "out there" with the sense of shelter "in here." Inside a community people trust each other, understand each other, and are never strangers to each other. They help and support each other, listen with sympathy, and forgive when forgiveness is needed. According to Bauman, this evocation of community stands for the kind of world that many people long for but that is not available and probably never was. It is a paradise lost, a nostalgic evocation of an imagined better past in which social relations were warm and harmonious. Used in this way, community becomes associated with a hope for something better than we have now.

Against this background, a study by Valerie Walkerdine (2010) highlights the potential tension between a deeply felt attachment to community and the contingency of that community's existence on its relationship with the outside world. She researched the sense of "communal beingness" in a large working-class community in South Wales, which was traumatized by the closure of its steelworks. She offers a dynamic view of community that emphasizes the importance of social networks and the relationality of social processes associated with community, especially when it is approached through the lived experience of people in that community. She criticizes most social science approaches to community for neglecting the emotional ties and affective economies that bind people together and proposes instead "the centrality of affect for understanding how people sharing a locality may be held together, in other words how communal being-ness might work" (95). The people Walkerdine interviewed talked about the community as being like a family held together, in part, by their attachment to the steelworks. Although the particular actions, feelings, objects, and places will be different, Walkerdine's affective-relational analysis of what holds people together in South Wales may have something to offer to participatory projects in HCI.

At first glance, there could be fewer communities apparently more redolent of Walkerdine's value of belonging and Bauman's notion of safety "in here" than a convent community. The Prayer Companion project (Gaver, Blythe, Boucher, Jarvis, Bowers, and Wright 2010) engaged with a settled community of nuns to design something that would help connect them with the concerns of the world outside their convent. As members of an enclosed order, prayer is central to the life of the convent in which this small group of elderly nuns lives, and they observe prayerful silence among themselves for most of each day. Because they are an enclosed order they have minimal, controlled engagement with the outside world but at the same time they recognize the centrality of the outside world to the meaning of their prayer lives. They thus want their prayer to be "pertinent" and to bring people "into the Presence of God."

Although the nuns saw the value of some knowledge of what was going on in the world, they were also eager not to upset the meaning of enclosure and what was important to them as a community or to upset each other in the process. It was clear that whatever changes would occur during, and as a result of, the project could only happen after careful negotiation with those nuns in the order who could engage directly with the research team on behalf of their community. So the research began with one member of the team (Mark Blythe) making many extended visits to the convent to try to understand what it was like to live in the convent and reporting back to the rest of the team before introducing other members. The main point of contact with the community was through Sister Peter, the "extern" sister, who is not fully enclosed and whose role involves being the main point of contact between the other sisters and the outside world. Her patient, in-depth explanations of the sisters' life of prayer were very important. The mother abbess and the mother vicaress also took part in a series of interviews over the two years of the project. This was followed by the development of a workbook of design ideas, which members of the team explored with the nuns. The aesthetics of the design ideas had been very carefully considered for the context of the convent and the prayer room; nevertheless, a number were rejected by the nuns as being too large and intrusive in the life of the convent. As the project team met and got to know the nuns, it became clear that the aim of the project was to allow the community of nuns to extend their reach but on their own terms. The challenge was to redistribute the sensible without disturbing community life, which involved agreeing to a precise balance between engagement with others outside the community and enclosure.

The design that was eventually deployed in the convent was a small T-shaped cross called the Prayer Companion, which could be placed fairly discretely on a hall table. A moving stream of text was displayed on top of the horizontal part of the T. The text consisted of a stream of headlines from a variety of news sites mixed with short sentences from wefeelfine. com, a site that crawls social network sites to collect statements beginning with "I feel." The mix was intended to balance the collective and global news headlines with some more personal and idiosyncratic messages that would give the nuns a sense of the lived experience of particular people to carry with them in their prayer.

There are a number of aspects of the Prayer Companion project that make it a particularly interesting example of a community participatory project. The attention of the design team to the experience of living in a settled community highlights the everyday interactions, care for each other, imagination, and focused activity that made this particular community. This convent is a very particular example of distribution of the sensible in which participants in the community live to rules of silence and enclosure that curtail their everyday engagement with others to the point, for example, at which the design team speak to and hear from the community through a very small number of them. For the nuns, this configuration of modes of perception and participation is designed to heighten their sensibility to being in the presence of God. Recognition of the nuns' eagerness to protect their order and their prayer life, even while trying to enrich it by connecting with the outside world, highlights tensions in their particular distribution of the sensible.

In the Prayer Companion project, exploring how the nuns would reconfigure their participation involved negotiating with those sisters who spoke on behalf of the rest of the community to work out ways of engaging with the needs of the wider world while also respecting and protecting the needs of their own community, especially the atmosphere of prayer that sustained the community. They were negotiating with the wisdom of a settled community that appreciated the lived experience and meanings that sustained them. They understood the importance of protecting what was precious to them while also extending their reach. So although the nuns were positive about the Prayer Companion, describing how it had prompted them to pray for particular events, nevertheless, there was an overriding sense that it could take them some years before they would be sure of its value to them. When participation reaches into areas where identity, agency, control, and self-determination are negotiated over time, then framings of experience become subject to the gravitational pull of belonging. But not all communities are as singular as an enclosed order of nuns.

Other projects pay more attention to the multiple, hybrid, and transient aspects of community. Later in this chapter, we will discuss a project that enquired into community participation among older people living in residential care and another that is enquiring into participation in a women's center, where women access support after leaving abusive relationships. Both explore issues of diversity and permeability within and between communities. The contexts in question draw attention to people who may be quite different from each other, with no history of shared values, practices, and identity, working out ways of living together. This involves developing frames of understanding, participating, and being that work for the people involved. In both cases, researchers negotiate entry into the community as people who are working out how to be and belong (or not) in the community, quite a different prospect from that experienced by the Prayer Companion team. Before we discuss these projects, we describe some conceptual resources for understanding belonging in such communities, which we have found in the work of Diane Hodges and Elspeth Probyn.

Belonging and Participating

Diane Hodges (1998) defines participation "as a way of belonging" in community and reflects on her own dilemma participating in a community of trainee teachers. Her dilemma involved living on a boundary between belonging and not belonging in a fairly settled, institutionalized community of teacher training. She was the only lesbian in her peer group and she felt that the difference between her and the other women was reinforced daily in her different dress, the fact that she didn't have a husband or boyfriend to talk about, her lack of interest in fashionable appearance, and her questioning attitude. Her encounters with her peer group became encounters with her fear of being found out. Her difference extended to identification with children over whom her tutors expected her to exercise authority. Hodges's experience of participating with misgivings embodies the experience of uncomfortable friction between belonging and autonomy. For, as well as referring to the bonds that tie people together, community is also used to express values, and, in order to belong, Hodges felt she would have had to compromise her values.

Hodges's reflection on her experience builds on and responds to Lave and Wenger's (1991) analysis of participation in communities of practice, an analysis that has been influential and appropriated in a variety of ways in studies of people's experiences of technology in community settings. Lave and Wenger analyze communities of practice in "processual historical terms" in which participation necessarily changes over time as people move from peripheral to central positions. The metaphor of moving from the periphery to the center is used by Lave and Wenger to conceptualize learning in a socially situated way. According to this conceptualization, learning is usefully construed in terms of movement between different forms of participation in community, for example, from the uncertain, unskilled, marginal participation of watching, questioning, and waiting to be shown to the assured participation of the skilled situated performer. This movement is not just from unskilled to skilled but also, and perhaps more important, is movement from being marginal with respect to the other members to being centrally one of them, a shift of identity in practice, a practical, relational transformation that takes place in people's sense of who they are and who they are becoming, understood in terms of the quality of their participation in the community. This quality of legitimate participation evokes the sense of belonging that is associated with confident membership.

Hodges's experience suggests that Lave and Wenger's ontology of participation in community needs to be elaborated to account for "moments when participation is organised by structures of privilege that deny difference and diversity" (Hodges 1998, 278). She describes these moments as "lags" in participation where the person is "doing" what is expected but is not identifying with the practice. Although engaged in the practices that signal legitimate membership, participants may feel marginalized or alienated from those practices, experiencing the conflict that Bauman highlighted between the desire to be in community and the feeling of not being entirely at home in community. Although the ontology of participation has often been taken up as describing clear movement from margin to center, Lave and Wenger recognized that there were many forms of participating stating, for example, that "there may well be no such thing as 'central participation' in a community of practice" (35). And yet they state that legitimate peripheral participation crucially involves "both absorbing and being absorbed in—the 'culture of practice'" (95). Over time participants are expected to make the culture of practice theirs. Whether definitive or explanatory in Lave and Wenger's ontology, the idea of movement from margins to center is at odds with Rancière's (1991) conceptualization of participation and learning. His commitment to an opening assumption of equality in dialogue, based on an approach to subjects' capacity rather than incapacity, resists notions of learning as moving toward a teacher or participation as moving toward a community ideal. For Rancière, learning is more mutual and reciprocal than that. The idea of needing to move from margins to center in order to belong entails a kind of established order with the potential to include or exclude. In its place, Rancière sees every form of subjectivization as a form of disidentification, which resonates with Hodges's resolution of her personal dilemma (Dasgupta 2008, 75).

Hodges's experience as outsider in a teacher training program foregrounds conceptual tensions between the expectation of appropriating a culture of practice and the acceptance of a multitude of ways of participating and the lived experience of conflict between wanting to be part of a community and yet feeling alienated from that community. Although she desperately wants to be a teacher, she wonders how she could possibly become absorbed in this community of practice when she feels seriously alienated from its dominant heteronormative relations and its construction of childhood, which betrays her own experience of early childhood education. To appropriate that culture of practice would require her to deny her lesbian identity and withdraw from the embodied conflict between her participation as child and as teacher, an act of betrayal as far as Hodges is concerned. Hodges's experience involves moments of disidentification and nonparticipation, belonging and participation:

> Nonparticipation constitutes an identificatory moment where a person is accommodating in participation and yet is experiencing an exclusion from any "normative" or unproblematic identification with practice. Quite crucially, nonparticipation describes conflict in the space between activity and identification, where there is a moment of multiplicitous identifications or *identificatory possibilities*. (Hodges 1998, 272–273)

A key point for Hodges then is that one can take part without feeling a sense of belonging. She sees such moments as ruptures between what people are actually doing and how they find themselves positioned in the community. Her account adds experiential weight to Rancière's suggestion that subjectivization is a form of disidentification and to Bauman's challenge to mythologized community nostalgia. It draws specific attention to an assumption of homogeneity of belonging and uniformity of movement in normative models of participation. People on the inside share certain qualities and characteristics that outsiders need to acquire before they too can belong. Movement toward the center of community is figured as a process of gradually becoming like and feeling like those notionally at the center, a hard-won equation of similarity with equality.

We started our discussion of participation in community by reflecting on the reification of community as an already established and settled form. Bauman critiqued a particularly nostalgic version at the heart of which is an imagined better past in which social relations were settled and harmonious. He saw it as appealing to a vision of community that never actually existed. Although it could easily be mistaken for a nostalgic throwback, a project that engaged with the singular belonging of enclosed nuns in a convent turned out to be critically productive. Their interest in connecting with the outside world without entering into it opened up a number of distinctive experiences of participating in community, which were developed in slightly different ways in Hodges's analysis of her experience of taking part without feeling a sense of belonging. Hodges's attention to the affective-relational aspects of community illustrated the depth of feeling that can be involved when participation creates tension in the affective economy. Something new emerges when somebody like Hodges feels at odds with the prevailing culture. Although this was not something she had bargained for, it is precisely what the nuns tried to manage in their negotiation of participating and not participating, identifying and not identifying. Addressing these complexities in communal living requires some way of thinking about the variety of modes of belonging in community, including multiple and "inbetween" belongings.

"Inbetween" Belongings

Elspeth Probyn's (1996) account of living in a Montreal neighborhood suggests a variety of genres or forms of what she calls *outside belongings* that may offer an alternative to normative assumptions about belonging. Instead of accepting the normality of the belonging insider, she plays around with plural outside belongings that happily accept and work with difference. Probyn foregrounds a changing, moving configuration of relations, through which, by coincidence rather than inclusion or exclusion, different ways of getting along together and different forms of belonging are articulated. As well as pointing to the plurality and sociality of belonging, Probyn's emphasis on outside belongings describes her method of surfacing, or making sensible, the social relations that bring belonging about.

Probyn describes the minuteness of social life on the tiny balconies of the old working class Montreal neighborhood in which she lived. In her area, as soon as spring arrived, balconies became the places where people spent most of their time at home. People lived on the outside for the summer in close proximity to neighbors yet also drawing new frontiers. There, Probyn would sometimes talk to her neighbors and at other times they all proceeded as if they were alone in private walled gardens, the boundary between conversation and privacy marked by what she thinks of as an inaudible rhythm of engaging with and tuning out. In this outside belonging, people learned to engage and to disengage, to participate in the social life of the community and to be invisible or hard of hearing when appropriate. Probyn's outside belonging finds ways to participate in community while respecting people's space, difference, and singularity, ignoring what is visible or audible for the greater good of the community. *Outside belonging* describes a surface or a space on which social relations are produced and made visible. In the Montreal example, though they are close and intimate, social relations create subtle manners of responding to what is made visible and audible by neighbors.

For Probyn, "the experience of quite literally living on the outside during the summer months ... speaks of something more than the term *identity* can catch, a cohabitation that goes beyond the limited concept of tolerance" (Probyn 1996, 5). Her Montreal neighborhood is a site for exploring "how individuals conjugate difference into manners of being, and how desires to become are played out in different circumstances" (5). It exemplifies a movement toward belonging, a kind of *becoming-other* in Probyn's eyes, which happens as different and distinct people, genders, generations, classes, or ethnicities are brought together and hang out together. So for Probyn, belonging involves a strong orientation toward other, a reconfiguration of social relationships marked by growing identification with other, while enacting "relationships of differentiation, of creation, of innovation" (Foucault 1984, 28). This is quite different to Hodges's experience of belonging in a teacher-training program connoting identification only, a quite different distribution of the sensible with no room for difference and innovation. Probyn's concept of outside belonging is an expression on the surface of the dialogical space we talked about in chapter 4. Equality in difference is a value that guides a moment-to-moment interaction. The balcony space is a forward-looking dialogical space on which those who live together, and who appreciate their difference, use their judgment and imagination to create an open, sometimes ambiguous, space for going on together.

The moments and movements of difference in which social relations are configured and reconfigured, particularly in the context of this discussion of the articulation of belonging and participation, are surfaced and become visible in outside belonging. Whereas models of participation that emphasize linear movement from exterior to interior or margin to center set up a hierarchy and imagine a preferred state of being on the inside or at the center, in outside belonging each moment and movement, no matter what the direction, suggests relational potential. Gestures that manage visibility in the community—a plant, a screen, or simply sitting facing in one direction and not the other—speak of orientation and preference, the desire to hear and be heard, see and be seen, or not. And they are all interesting, not just those that move in a predefined direction, because articulations of becoming in the community and of the varieties of belonging that play out in community participation.

Probyn describes a moving, changing distribution of the sensible that emerges from everyday interactions. It is not the policed distribution of social order that Rancière sets up as the sometimes focus of dissent but a locally and implicitly negotiated partition of the sensible. Recall from chapter 4 Rancière's community of sense, "a certain cutting out of space and time that binds together practices, forms of visibility, and patterns of intelligibility" (Rancière 2009b, 31). In Probyn's neighborhood, space was made by neighbors, who got on together, managing the sensible to indicate their preferences and desires at particular times, in the expectation based on experience that those preferences would be respected.

The desire to belong, to be part of the community, and at the same time recognizing and respecting the importance of difference and the inevitability of differentiation, produces a variety of relations and relationships among individuals and groups. In this case, finding innovative ways of belonging hinges on recognizing the importance of also not belonging and requires of individuals who live on that threshold to "conjugate difference into manners of being" (Probyn 1996, 5). For Probyn, the desire to belong in a situation that values difference is the social force that reconfigures those social relationships.

Desire is productive; it is what oils the lines of the social; it produces the pleats and folds which constitute the social surface we live. It is through and with desire that we figure relations of proximity to others and other forms of sociality.... The desire to belong propels, even as it rearranges, the relations into which it intervenes. (Probyn 1996, 13)

There is a movement and fluidity to social relations and participation described by Probyn and Hodges, a crisscrossing inevitability when the desire to belong is mixed with the desire to be outside. It cuts through the categorial straightjacket created by normative constructions of belonging that create a dichotomy between belonging and not belonging to create varieties of "ongoing inbetweenness" (Probyn 1996, 6) that render outside belongings plural.

In the context of participating in community, "inbetweenness" draws attention to the rhetorical and experiential constrictions of the conventional categorial approach to belonging in community. We have to conjure up a clumsy new word to articulate ways of belonging that are other than the conventional, "inbetween" the categories of insider and outsider, marginal and central, identification and differentiation, belonging and identity. The very desire to belong already places us on the outside. Moreover, as Probyn recognizes, "the processes of belonging are always tainted with deep insecurities about the possibility of truly fitting in, of even getting in" (40). Finding a way to belong in-between when institutional pressures pull and push conformity is the challenge. It is not all Balconyville, as Probyn is first to recognize. Indeed, for Hodges, living in-between legitimate central participation and her own embodied peripherality was too difficult. Living on the threshold was a painful betrayal of her embodied past.

Belonging "inbetween" is where Rancière's commitment to different yet equal really matters. By making sensible the reasonableness of people being different, it challenges any attempts to define participation in terms of similarity to account for their unreasonableness. Rancière's invocation of equality in difference as a starting assumption when interpreting and framing experience is a challenge to normative accounts of socialization into community that deny diversity and socially engaged accounts of full participation as requiring performance. Hodges's experience of alienation performing into a community of practice adds an experiential layer to the challenge that places moments of disidentification and nonparticipation in an embodied personal history that resists betrayal.

Having a Say and Having a Voice

Hodges's experience and Rancière's problematization of the value of the alignment of equality and community challenge the privileging of community that can be seen in much contemporary art, activism, and political discourse on civic engagement and collaboration. Although the practical benefits and costs of prosaic communal living are clear to most people living in cities, villages, religions, and professions, reification of community runs the risk of nostalgically hankering after an idealized better past rather than throwing light on the present and imagining a future. A dialogical approach to community collaboration opens up the possibility of a critical design commitment to community that is creative and inclusive rather than nostalgic and exclusive. It does this by arguing that the *voice* in dialogue is *constitutive*. *Having a say,* as participants such as Hodges may have had, enables people in community to express themselves and reproduces meanings and feelings that existed independently of community interaction. *Having a voice* goes beyond having a say by creating new understandings that were not available prior to the encounter (Deetz and Simpson 2004). A dialogic approach, which treats the voices of diverse participants as constitutive, has the potential to render community collaboration radical and generative. Seeing communities as constituted by the voices of those participating in them is a theoretically significant shift from the nostalgic yearning for stable, cohesive community that could be a significant design aspiration for community-centered projects.

The value of a dialogical approach to community can be seen in the work of WochenKlauser, a group of Austrian artists whose artistic practice involves intervening in communities to bring about the kinds of transformative participation that Till described in chapter 4. Kester (2004) describes one of their projects, which clearly involves bringing different voices in the community, who usually do not hear each other, together. In this project they brought drug-addicted women who had turned to prostitution to support their habit, local politicians, journalists, and activists together on dozens of boat trips on Lake Zurich over several weeks to talk to each other about the issue of drug addiction and to come up with some way of addressing it. Facilitating dialogue between groups in a community who have distinct voices on life in that community, voices that would generally be at odds with each other, and who have a stake in being heard, hardly evokes nostalgic cohesive community. Indeed it might be more useful to see it as potential community emerging from dialogue between new configurations of voices, when that new configuration taps into relational potential in the interactions between people. In this case it also resulted in a modest concrete response to the problem, the creation of a small boarding house where drug-addicted sex workers could have a safe place to sleep and to access health and other services.

WochenKlauser's dialogical practice creates spaces in which distinctly different voices are brought together in a commitment to action. The potential to transform or even simply energize community is in the challenging and questioning dialogue that brings about new understandings and social action. A generative approach to community as something to be worked at rather than something given provides a critical lens on community-centered design projects. It most directly challenges assumptions that community can be formed or energized by design interventions that simply bring different parts of an existing community together to *have their say*. Projects that operate from these assumptions provide opportunities for people to express themselves without necessarily bringing about any new understanding. They create roles within an existing frame but, because they don't perturb the frame, they do so without any redistribution of the sensible. For many such projects, dialogue between participants is a means to the end of simply bringing people together. Aspects of the Bespoke project described previously were like this. They were largely geared toward giving the people of Callon and Fishwick a *say* in the hope that this would bring them together and bring about a renewed sense of community. By contrast, WochenKlauser redistribute the sensible by dissolving the frame that reinforces everybody's existing positions and creates a new frame in which all voices are assumed to be equal and different. This is a similar move to Asher's insistence on an egalitarian contract for the students in LACMA (Peltomäki 2010). Projects in which people have a voice, have the potential to create moments in which community can experience what Probyn describes as "a cohabitation that goes beyond the limited concept of tolerance" (1996, 5).

As Rancière (2006) describes it in *The Politics of Aesthetics,* the "apportionment of parts and positions is based on a distribution of spaces, times, and forms of activity that determines the very manner in which something in common lends itself to participation and in what way various individuals have a part in this distribution" (12). Probyn's approach to living together, as outside belongings that can be proximate and private, describes participation as negotiated on the surface where people work out over time and experience together what is sensible. As people move in and out of the community, they learn to give each other space and time. This is a setting in which the distribution of the sensible is an ongoing project of reconfiguration through histories of particular encounters and relationships, in which convivial living together works out *manners of being* together. This is in contrast with an imposed distribution that controls what is sensible (to whom) and "who can have a share in what is common to the community based on what they do and on the time and space in which this activity is performed" (Rancière 2006, 12), the kind of distribution that Hodges's categorial analysis suggests occurred in her teacher training and also that WochenKlauser suggests was happening in Zurich before their intervention. WochenKlauser brought together two communities of sense in which people engaged in *forms of activity* such as drug taking and politics operate in different spaces and times and tend not to participate together in anything common. The intervention created a space in which they could hardly avoid participating in common.

We can see from WochenKlauser's projects, and indeed from Asher's installations earlier, that one of the roles design and art can play in the redistribution of the sensible is to make alternative participative experiences possible and, in the process, alternative modes of participation sensible. By designing something for the nuns to help them become aware of the experiences and concerns of people outside the convent, the Prayer Companion project may also be seen to contribute to a redistribution of the sensible in that particularly settled context by making alternative experiences of participation available. In the participatory projects that will be the focus of much of the remainder of this chapter, the communities are less settled than in Prayer Companion and less democratic and proactive than in Probyn's balcony community. The very desire to belong, which according to Probyn propels sociality and participation, is not always present. As we shall see, if design is to successfully mediate participation in such communities it has to address tensions between collective and individual, and perhaps also between belonging and betrayal, in a further renegotiation of what it can mean to participate in community. These tensions raise questions about the complexity of participation in community when the individuals involved fight against or are suspicious of the forms of belonging implied by the very term *community.*

When people come to live together due to circumstances outside of their control, for example, declining health or independence, developing new relational practices may be a regular reminder of betrayal to them. When people come to be together in a community group or center that is other to them because of dissatisfaction with what they have or because of fear of not belonging, the irreducibility of their individuality may present them with difficulties when it comes to opening up to others in the *new community.* The idea that there is any new community for them when their experience is so in-between has to be questioned. In these examples, the questions that are raised can be seen in terms of lived experience of communal practices and the problems that must exist in these circumstances for participant and researchers in even representing community. This latter issue is particularly salient in the Jacob House project, in which a great deal of time and effort had to be invested in negotiating entry to the field and working out roles for participants and researchers.

Belonging in a Residential Home for Older People

The Jacob House project, along with the Prayer Companion project described previously, was developed as part of the United Kingdom's New Dynamics of Aging Initiative. As we mentioned in chapter 3, Jacob House was a council-funded residential care home for elderly people in which one of the major challenges for the project team was encouraging residents and staff to participate in the project. To oil the wheels of relationship building, Mark Blythe, the ethnographer who first approached Jacob House, developed some "tickets to talk" (Sacks 1992, 195). Tickets to talk provide a way of starting a conversation. For example, walking a dog in a park may be a good excuse to talk to other people walking their dogs. A mix of the following was used: introducing residents to Google Earth and asking them about the places they had lived in order to encourage them to reminisce; showing residents online photographs of the city to provoke them to tell stories about their lives in the city; inviting residents to play with digital novelties such as the iPhone Flickr app. They worked to some extent, breaking the ice and getting conversation going, sometimes for a limited duration. However, when they went on for a longer time, the engagement was often very tiring for residents.

By chance, Mark knew an artist who had worked in a care home previously and who was interested in getting involved again. Feeling that it would create opportunities for a social encounter with residents during which silence and rest would also be natural, Phil, the artist, began to make some portraits of residents. This enabled lasting, sometimes intimate, engagement in which silence, conversation, and observation could all occur fairly easily for everybody involved without straining the residents. This activity grew, with two other artists joining in and an art club from a local school also becoming regular visitors. When a collection of portraits had been made, they became a traveling exhibition and were later installed in the care home itself, where the public was allowed to visit to see them during set times.

The process of entering the community and developing roles in this project deserves some attention in terms of participation as belonging in community. The art projects created space for residents and team members to develop roles for themselves with which they could be comfortable, in which the residents had a say, and through which they could sometimes give voice to their sense of themselves. The residents were generally quite happy with the artists visiting and painting them and the place in which they lived. Although they might occasionally be self-conscious about it, they could relax, chat a bit, and enjoy the company. If they were not in the mood for it, they did not join in. There is something more clearly negotiated about this arrangement than there would have been with a series of interviews that may not have been discussed individually with them before the project began. Some of the residents also allowed one of the artists, a photographer, to take pictures of them in their rooms and afterward some had those pictures framed and displayed in their rooms. This suggests a degree of comfort with these project activities when you consider that their room is the only near-private space that the residents had.

Is it too much to claim that the residents may have also had a voice in the development and sense making around these projects? From a dialogical perspective, people know that they have a voice, not when they express themselves, but when others respond to them. If they are ignored or treated superficially, they know that their contribution—and in community that means themselves—is not valued. They know that they are not expected to participate. The response that recognizes the worth of another starts with active listening: listening to the other person, to the situation from which their contributions come, and to their otherness and distinctiveness. It does not seem too far-fetched to suggest that the art projects, the patient engagement of artists with residents as well as the lively company of the artists and the art club school children gave all participants the opportunity to sense their distinctiveness in this context.

Grant Kester (2004), in his analysis of an emerging dialogical aesthetic in contemporary art, is critical of a tendency among some relational artists to create social spaces that are insensitive to the situation of those for whom it is made. Dialogically, responsiveness is a defining quality of any utterance. It is when individuals are responsive or answerable to each other that dialogical or community moments occur. Whether it involves spoken word, art installation, or digital intervention, a responsive utterance is already marked by listening, even as it is made. An unresponsive utterance seems deaf to the experience and the situation of its audience. Listening, in this sense, is not one of a series of discrete moves in a pattern of information exchange; it is an aesthetic sensibility to the other in intersubjective, social, and cultural relations. Indeed, it could be understood as an affective commitment to the value of community and to the value of that particular community.

Having developed relationships with the residents, the team tried out a variety of technologies to see how residents and visitors might engage with them. One was a Video Window, which gave an extra view on the outside world from a camera placed on the roof of the home. Others involved organizing the portraiture work so that residents could be more active in the process. The team also experimented with public portraiture in which one of the artists painted on a tablet PC. His painting was projected onto a wall of the public lounge so that residents and visitors could see and comment on his work as it was being done. In a variation on this that the school children were very enthusiastic about, standing a person in front of the projector, made it possible for people who felt they had no artistic ability at all to color them in and produce a portrait quite quickly. Children painting each other in this way provided an engaging spectacle for residents and children alike, and some caregivers also became involved. In another variation, Flickr images of the area or of topics chosen by residents were projected onto a canvas hung in another room. They became a source of conversation and fun. The final technological legacy of this two-year project, the Photostroller, is a portable display that continually shows images from the Internet, some random and some related to categories selected by residents. In a follow-up visit some years after the project had ended it was still being used but by residents of another residential care home because Jacob House had closed down.

There is a very strong sense in which the main legacy and lessons of this project are in the relationships that the team built up with the residents and the patient, imaginative dialogue that enabled all involved to experience new ways of participating in community together. The team described it as follows:

> If we have succeeded at all in enhancing our participants' experience of ageing through technological interventions, it is not by observing users, identifying needs, goals and activities, then specifying the requirements of design solutions. It is by spending time, living with them a little, and by letting our relationship grow to a point where we could respond empathically with something. The form of response was less of a solution to a problem and more like a gift. (Blythe et al. 2010, 169)

The Jacob House project and setting was fluid in a number of ways. The project team recognized that the age of residents and the fact that some of them died during the project were salient aspects of lived experience in Jacob House. As elderly people, many of whom are unable to live independently, the residents live outside a society that valorizes independence. They must be sick of hearing about the problem and burden of an aging population. Some may feel betrayed by the state and society that sees them in that way and also by their own bodies and health for putting them into that position. Jacob House itself also turned out to be temporary. Although it was not an immediate issue during the project, it turned out that Jacob House would close a couple of years later. The residents were moved to other council-funded homes in the area. Knowing that this could happen at any time—could happen *to* you, not that you decide to make it happen—has to be unsettling. In the height of adapting to their changing health and circumstances, they are also expected to live together with others whom they have not chosen as neighbors in a community that is always in between living and dying, being and gone. And, for those who live long enough, when economic or demographic circumstances change, the community and dialogical space that they have helped create and come to terms with is dismantled by the state and they have to start again. With such pervasive uncertainty, each concrete, particular person in the residential home has to find his or her own way of being together for a while with others, whom he or she has not chosen.

Similar to Probyn and her neighbors, the residents live an "inbetween" life, in which personal space is marked out and public space acknowledged. Also similar to Probyn and her balcony community, their belonging is outside and temporary. Unlike Probyn's experience, outside belonging is not pleasant for many of the residents of Jacob House. They are outside the homes that many of them would have cared for over years and outside the neighborhoods and communities that they had been part of all that time. For older residents in a residential care home, "outside" may be an existential way of being and belonging. We have referred to Probyn's *outside belonging* a number of times already in this chapter but there is something about lived experience in residential care that makes it real and that shows a potential shadow side to Probyn's generally optimistic approach. Probyn's outside belonging was influenced by Agamben's short philosophical meditation on community in which the notion of the outside is rendered as a passage or a threshold. Agamben (1993) captures the sense of outside belonging as follows:

The threshold is not, in this sense, another thing with respect to limit; it is, so to speak, the experience of the limit itself, the experience of being-*within* an outside. (67)

At a time when their singularity—the event of their being and of their difference in being (Nancy 2001) —must be a pressing matter for some of them, when many of their friends and companions are unwell or dying, when their own mortality is made sensible to them, and their sense of being inside at home is threatened, they also have to deal with belonging. Empathy requires a fierce act of dialogical, creative, imaginative understanding when the focus of that empathy is so fiercely other. This is also the case in our next project, a feminist participatory art research project that uses photo sharing to try to understand the experiences of women accessing support after leaving an abusive relationship.

Creating Space with Survivors of Domestic Violence

Sociality can be very difficult for people who have experienced domestic violence. The experience can have profound impacts on their confidence, self-esteem, communication, sense of security, and relationships. Rachel Clarke and colleagues (Clarke, Wright, Balaam, and McCarthy 2013) are running a participatory project to explore the process of rebuilding lives for women who have experienced domestic violence. The project is based in a center at the heart of a large immigrant community, which focuses on black, Asian, and minority ethnic women's development through holistic support based on understanding the social and political context of immigration and the women's particular histories and backgrounds. The project involved the main researcher, Rachel Clarke, spending one day a week in the center.

Rachel entered the center by volunteering for three months to get to know the staff and the women before any decisions would be made about the project. She took part in cooking club sessions a couple of days a week and in taster art sessions one day a week. This turned out to be a very useful way of addressing the women's caution about newcomers and an understandable guardedness among the center management. Although all the women had recently left abusive relationships, they did not necessarily know each other and some of them also had concerns for anonymity and privacy given their circumstances, so it took them a while to feel comfortable with each other and with Rachel. It also became clear during this time that whereas the women were taking part because they wanted to, they did not necessarily want to be compliant to leadership or to work as a group.

After she had completed her time as a volunteer, Rachel, the staff of the center, and some of the other researchers decided that participatory arts workshops would be a useful way of supporting connection among the women in the group. Photo sharing was seen as a potentially socially enriching practice that could support interaction. It was thought that the women would be able to construct identity and build relationships through sharing stories with each other around photographs and video sequences. The team was aware that photographs, especially of family and other aspects of personal life, could also be emotionally challenging and raise issues of security and physical safety for people who have experienced domestic violence.

Some of the photographs that were brought to the workshop expressed and affirmed aspects of women's sense of self in new relationships that were important to them. They articulated clear and distinctive voices that belonged to the community in a variety of ways and that were also edging away from it as their sense of independence developed and they began to feel they could move on. The dialogical space supported by the workshops enabled women to participate in their own ways and to negotiate their relationships with each other and with the community as they participated. And, although most of the women share a history in the center together, their distinctive ways of belonging—inside, outside, on the threshold, managing the balance between privacy and sharing, individually and together— shows a dynamic ongoing reconfiguration of participation as the women rebuild their lives.

For example, Zahrah and Saeeda brought in albums containing photos of their time together on days out with the center and with their children. The albums were almost identical. They contained pictures of the same outings, the only difference being that they were taken from slightly different angles. In some of the photographs they were wearing the same outfits.

Saeeda and Zahrah used the photographs to illustrate how they felt about their relationship with one another from joint and individual perspectives. They found it difficult to put together what they wanted to say about their friendship and asked Rachel for some help. Rachel sat with them for a while, talking to them about their friendship, asking each of them what they like about the other and how they would feel if they did not know each other. She asked them about wearing the same dress and coat and they told her about going shopping together and buying the same dresses to wear on a set day out. When Rachel asked them whether this was for themselves or others, they told her that they wanted to let people know that they have had the same experience and have come from the same place. They talked about the similarity in their journeys and experiences.

In text they wrote together to accompany the photos, they described their relationship in terms of the strength and support they gave one another and what they had in common through sharing the same experiences. They described meeting two years earlier in a women's refuge and feeling freedom for the first time. They also described each from the other's perspective as loving, helpful, and supportive, and as always there for one another:

I would feel lonely and quiet without Saeeda being around.
She [Zahrah] makes me feel strong when we are together. (2522)

The photographs and the text collectively illustrate an ongoing commitment to what they felt was important to them, their friendship as a reflection of self, as if the event of coming-into-presence to themselves as individuals coexisting, and as a mutually supportive couple, provides a foundation for going forward. But the sense of participation in community also involving times in which distance from others is experienced can also be seen and heard in the expressions of exclusiveness in the photographs and in the need for the other to ground an emerging confidence to move on.

Many of the women addressed in the workshop the intricate management of being both singular and plural. Five of the six women had developed and maintained strong supportive relationships while staying in a refuge together. The workshop provided space for further coming together as a group as well as opportunities to explore together a sense of moving on and becoming more independent. For example Huzna created a sequence she called her "Life Journey," which consisted of photos of family and friends when she was young, pictures of the refuge that she had stayed at, her new home, her children, and her sewing. She used the images and the sequences to describe to others how she was preparing for the future. When she shared the DVD in the final session, her photographs evoked reminiscences from the others about the refuge. Huzna's sharing copies with people outside the group was seen as a sign of her strength and growing independence.

It is hardly surprising that women who had been abused would be careful about anonymity and privacy. However the sharing practices that were negotiated through the workshops demonstrated subtle and varied preferences that balanced a willingness to share with a need for privacy and anonymity. For example, Huma, who preferred working privately in the sessions, made a video called the "Last Leaf of Hope" in which she used photographs of a leafless tree with an animated falling leaf to express her feelings of sadness. Initially she did not want to share it with the rest of the group whom she felt might not understand her feelings and might mock her. When talking to Rachel about her images and video she told her that she was more understanding than the others. By the later sessions, she had added more images to create a more hopeful narrative. In week seven, she wrote the following to accompany her images.

When I'm in darkness, it's very hard to manage life. There is the last leaf of hope, everything will be OK. When it falls down we are also broke. But the new horizon of hope is alive in us. All joys of life will come. (2523)

As has been the case with a number of the projects we have discussed, one of the major challenges and foci of the Women's Centre project has been creating space in which participants feel that they can define themselves to others in the context of the project. Rachel's decision to begin by volunteering played an important part in meeting that challenge in this project, enabling her to get to know the staff and the women in ways that a straight-up invitation to participate in a research project might never have allowed. The sensitive use of photo-sharing workshops to construct a space in which the women could create the stories that they wanted to tell, stories that did not have to follow a specific narrative form, and stories that, as it turned out, could tell of the shared experiences of two women as well as the unique experiences of other individuals also contributed to the responsive self-expression that became apparent through the workshops. Photo sharing at the Women's Centre resonates with the informal portrait painting sessions that took place Jacob House, creating opportunities for the kind of convivial presence needed to bring the experience of community to life. It would seem from all three projects in this chapter that designing for community belonging requires a presence from the project team or at least the key people on site, which is quite different from the formal presence of researcher or designer. The participants in the Women's Centre and in Jacob

House might have felt alienated from research but took part in creative and playful practices that they could engage with or not as they wished and bring their own creativity to bear as they desired.

This form of participation is a step beyond Till's transformative participation discussed in chapter 4, which requires a reimagination of expert knowledge in terms of user experience. Instead, it requires a reimagination of the ways in which researchers and participants are present to each other, a redistribution of the sensible that reconfigures the social order that would usually be expected in research projects and design enquiries. It involves reimagining *being* together by being together. Following Tim Ingold's (2013, 3) clarification of the differences between ethnography and anthropology, the participatory projects in this chapter have involved researchers being with participants and learning from them ways to carry on that expand human potential in their particular communities. At its best, this form of participation sharpens the modes of perception and modes of participation of all involved.

Making Space for Dialogue through In-between Belongings

In the projects that we discussed in chapter 4, participation was mediated by an orientation toward concrete, named others with personal histories, hopes, and desires. In the projects described in this chapter this orientation is reinforced but the process is played out in social contexts in which experiences such as belonging, identification, and disidentification are heightened. For much of this chapter, we have been exploring aspects of belonging and participating in community, aware that the very idea of community is a powerful draw and a problematic concept. Probyn's outside belonging opened up a space for us to consider participation in these contexts as plural, complex, and heterogeneous.

Entry into community can be a challenging proposition for any outsider and, as one of the researchers commented to us, it can invoke a response that makes them feel as if they are from Mars. This speaks to a pervasive sense of belonging within community even when belonging is approximate and outside. Even when there are many ways of belonging and being in community such as Jacob House and the Women's Centre—those who belong in community can easily spot those who do not. When researchers are framed as entering community to gather information from informants, it creates a rift between "them" and "us" that has to be closed before any creative space of mutual interest to researcher and participants can be constructed.

In Jacob House and the Women's Centre, artistic practices played an important part in making a creative space of mutual interest. In Jacob House, this came about as a pragmatic and serendipitous response to the challenge of engaging when participants were not particularly interested in or welcoming of research. In the Women's Centre, it was a more knowing approach based on the researcher and staff's previous experience in community arts projects. In the Women's Centre, arts practice offered a form of engagement that enabled participants to exercise their creativity and their agency in choosing whether to take part or not.

In both projects, making and sharing art together facilitated a playfulness that would otherwise be absent and a self-expression and sharing that would otherwise be pointed and probably very difficult. But in the Women's Centre it was more than just a ticket to talk. The art practice created a space for people to reflect differently about themselves and their lives, encouraging them to look forward rather than backward, to focus on the hope of things to come rather than the regret of things that were. Exploring unfamiliar ways of self-expression can be liberating in the right context, and the researchers in both projects created contexts in which people were prepared to have a go. They stripped out the formality that can accompany an invitation to share your story, which in a research, performance, or therapeutic setting can be daunting. They enabled people to talk about their experiences while sitting for a painter or painting and to share their experiences in their own way through photographs. In doing so, the researchers changed their own conventional relationships with informants or participants. They became present to participants in a way that was appreciative of their creativity and willingness to trust that it would lead somewhere interesting. Engaging with the vitality of other people's creativity—in art and in everyday discourse—makes space for them to be singular and plural and for the relationship to acknowledge shared experience and distance. Participation here—in this case the participation of the researchers in the communities—has to be negotiated and has to be based on a being-with that assumes equality from the outset and that shares difference between the people belonging in their communal space in their own approximate, outside ways.

While on the threshold, trying on new roles, researchers may have helped to reframe the dialogical space in Jacob House and the Women's Centre by dissolving frames that reinforce their existing positions and creating frames in which alternative ways of being, and being-with, could be explored. This shifts the focus from participation as identification to participation as approximate belonging or as exploring the vitality of being-together for a while. In these projects, researchers were facilitators or artists encouraging their participants to share in creative, expressive ways that were new to many of them. When people take part as novices in an arts-based workshop, they know that they are not expected to be experts and that they are invited to give it a go and learn from it without any expectation of producing an artwork. They also know that the artist facilitating the workshop is not there to show off his or her skill but to help participants to do as well as they can. This creates a relatively safe creative space in which recognition of the tension between participants' simultaneous experiences of being-with and shared distance gives vitality to being-together for a while. This kind of space is difficult to create and may be something that was lacking in the performance-based works such as Humanaquarium described in chapter 3, which are often associated with a public performance and a performer showing off skill and virtuosity.

Some artistic interventions into community operate in a more directive and interventionist way, trying to bring about concrete and lasting changes in community. We have seen how WochenKlauser bring people and resources together to make a concrete difference in their area or community. As well as the Lake Zurich project already described, their projects include a community development intervention in which they staged a series of conversations in a small town that resulted in the formation of three interest groups to develop proposals for change and collaboration with students that focused on redesigning their school space. WochenKlauser's projects are characterized by a period of intense dialogue for a limited amount of time (about eight weeks) to create a concrete intervention in the community.

Although they all reframe the space for dialogue and participation in one way or another, the WochenKlauser method is quite different from the Jacob House and Women's Centre approach to using artistic practice to facilitate dialogue, sharing experience, and energizing a sense of support and belonging. The Jacob House and Women's Centre projects are more interested in exploring forms of belonging with people whose outsideness opens up spaces for thinking about community as it might become. Their approaches, especially the Women's Centre project, resonate more with the work of artist Jeremy Deller.

In an essay in the catalog for *Joy in People*, Deller's 2012 retrospective exhibition, the cultural theorist Stuart Hall draws attention to Deller's political imaginary as animated by the idea "that people who are sometimes considered to be unimportant, or not worth listening to, matter. They are creative but often have their creativity denied or taken away from them …

they should be valued for what they are—their voices heard, their practices celebrated" (Hall 2012, 88–89). The pleasure in Deller's egalitarian political imaginary—the joy in people—can be seen in *Folk Archive,* an ongoing project that was started by Jeremy Deller and Alan Kane in 2000. Deller and Kane collect artwork created by people who would not primarily consider themselves artists. It includes work from prisoners and community groups, performers in Notting Hill Carnival, protestors, pop fans, and homeless people. The relationship between Deller and the artists in his *Folk Archive* collection is not a simple one. Deller is not just curious about British folk or vernacular art; he responds to it as an important expression of British local knowledge and social imagination.

Another of Deller's works, *The Battle of Orgreave,* was a day-long reenactment of a key event from the miners' strike in England in 1984. The strike lasted for over a year and was extremely divisive, splitting families, towns, and the union movement. One of the seminal events of the strike was a particularly violent confrontation between miners and the police at a British Steel coking plant in the village of Orgreave, South Yorkshire. The National Union of Mineworkers organized a mass picket of about five to six thousand people from across the country to blockade the Orgreave plant, and the police deployed a similar number of officers. The confrontation involved a series of pushes by the miners and mounted responses by the police. A forceful advance by the police, which included the use of batons, led to the miners being driven away from the plant and into the village. Stone throwing and further police use of batons followed, including examples of policemen attacking fleeing miners and hitting them with their batons. Deller recollects seeing this on television:

On 18 June 1984 I was watching the evening news and saw footage of a picket at the Orgreave coking plant in South Yorkshire in which thousands of men were chased up a field by mounted police. It seemed a civil war between the North and the South of the country was taking place in all but name. (Deller 2002, 7)

When civil war is invoked, the very idea of belonging and being-with is challenged. Deller's frustration at media misrepresentation of the Battle of Orgreave points to a political manipulation of the distribution of the sensible that was determined to conceal the positions and voices of miners in this battle. For example, recent newspaper articles report accusations of fabrication by the police of their evidence (*Guardian* 2012) and of inaccurate reporting involving reversing the order of events of the confrontation between police and miners by the BBC (BBC 2014). Deller's bold reenactment project made the social configuration of the time an open work that might lead to a redistribution of the sensible in the present.

About one thousand people took part in the reenactment of the battle, including about two hundred ex-miners and a small number of ex-policemen and ambulance men. Many of these had been involved in the original confrontation in Orgreave. The remaining eight hundred were from historical reenactment societies, who had experience of staging historical reenactments of events from outside their own living memory or experience. There was a day of rehearsal in advance of the event, in which participants practiced parts of the performance and told their own stories of the strike to each other.

For Deller, participation in *The Battle of Orgreave* involved an encounter with the past and present. By having former Orgreave workers, ex-policemen, reenactment society members, and Nottingham miners who had "scabbed" (crossed the picket lines) during the strike take part, Deller created a space in which the reenactment could support a fresh experience of the original event and personal histories and narratives could be made sensible and put in dialogue with each other. Reenacting the battle made sensible the people involved in the original event in ways that were subverted by government and media representations at the time. Imaginatively redistributing the sensible in the context of the desire of many to revisit their direct and mediated experience of the original was intended by Deller to enable participants to see afresh the battle and the wounds it had caused.

In *The Battle of Orgreave,* it is the multilayered, multithreaded, dissensual conversations between those involved in the reenactment that not only made the project possible but in many ways also define it. These conversations made visible the reciprocal exploratory relationships based on mutual interest and celebration that emerged as the project evolved. In *Folk Archive* and *The Battle of Orgreave,* Deller does not position himself as delegate or spokesman for folk artists or miners, a role that has occasionally been mooted for designers and user experience specialists in the design process. He does not speak for any of the communities involved. He laughs with the makers of humorous pieces, enjoys the insight of those who see something a little bit differently than others, identifies with the anger of those who feel cheated and robbed. He identifies and participates with them. But he also distances himself when he gives those participative responses an artistic form as participants speak for themselves in dialogue with each other and with him. Taken as a whole this dialogical encounter unfolds over time through processes of movement between a variety of intersubjective positions or perspectives, with participants discursively and imaginatively moving toward the experience of the other and then slightly away from the other's experience, standing apart better to see and be seen, feel and reflect on those feelings.

Deller's approach to these projects demonstrates how an ethic of generosity and respect—valuing the other as other, separate from self—makes space for dialogue in the context of strong artistic vision and leadership. And it is through dealing with such encounters, making sense of and accommodating them, that local knowledge and social imagination are produced. In Deller's work, the encounter for many participants is likely to be with Deller's particular response to their experience, history, and expertise. It seems from interviews and commentaries on his work, as well as from comments by participants during and after the projects, that Deller's practice is deeply respectful of local skill, knowledge, and experience, and that he builds many of his projects around his encounter with it.

Echoing chapter 3, one of the recurring themes in this chapter has been the otherness—sometimes intense otherness—of the people we live, work, and engage with. Probyn, Agamben, and others have given us the beginnings of a language to deal with experiences of outside or threshold belonging and the potentially alienating experience of being-with, even in community. Deller provides some insight into the potential for creative artistic and design encounter with otherness based on an ethic of appreciating and responding to difference from one's own center of value. We see his imaginative response to a feeling that he had had for a couple of decades that there had been an egregiously unfair telling of the story of Orgreave in the media at the time it happened. He finds a unique artistic response that enacts a dialogue with otherness. He ensures that it happens through the kind of engagement with all involved that establishes his good faith in the project. He gives them the field—the most evocative and creative space in this situation—and stands back.

In their different ways, each of the projects discussed in this chapter give participants the field. In each case, although never pretending to be other than they are, the project teams have followed the other trusting that the journey would lead them somewhere interesting. They have tried to find what the participants want to do or are good at doing and used that as a basis for design enquiry. Through engaging with residents who responded to the sociality of painting that enabled quiet time as well as a chat, creative activity as well as fun, they managed to negotiate a participatory space in among the imagination and values of the residents. Through creating an amiable space in which their experience and their privacy was respected, the team at the Women's Centre explored with women ways of looking back and looking forward, in sadness and in hope, individually and collectively. In each of these cases, as in Deller's projects, the value of living with contradiction and ambiguity instead of always trying to resolve it is demonstrated.

In the projects that we have discussed in this chapter, in consideration of varieties of belongings in community, the open creative space of previous chapters has gathered dimensions and perspectives, such as outside, threshold, and belonging, has become plural and approximate. Because these varieties of belongings have been explored through design enquiries, the need and indeed impulse to engage with participants wherever the sociality and imagination of the community took the project, has resulted in a pull to the vernacular in discourse and participation. The everyday languages and practices of older people living in Jacob House or in a convent, the everyday discourses and concerns of women who have been through the experience of domestic violence, and the prosaic creativity of folk artists and anger of ex-miners have been at the heart of this chapter. The varieties of approximate belongings in complex, sometimes divided, culturally and racially challenged societies have turned our attention throughout this chapter to the vernacular publics that defined the variety that we encountered in this chapter. In the next chapter, which looks at the final genre of participation, we will discuss the emergence of vernacular publics through social media.

6   Participating in Publics

In chapter 3, we began with an analysis of participation as a form of encounter with otherness that involves coming to terms with difference. Viewing these encounters as dialogical, that is, as open and unfinalized, is helpful in questioning assumptions about spectators, audiences, and users being passive consumers. Many of the projects discussed in chapter 3 involve staged encounters with otherness in which some new meaning is created and some new ways of imagining social experience are brought about. In these encounters, participants are expected to step out of their routine social relations and engage with others in ways that are experientially different and potentially transformative.

In chapter 4, we explored how in extended interpersonal dialogues between designer and users, the impulse toward design goes beyond the desire simply to provide solutions to problems already given, toward a commitment to redefine social arrangements, challenge institutional norms, and make new social relations possible. This laid the groundwork for an extension of our thinking about participation from a process of temporary engagement with others to include relationship building.

In chapter 5 on designing for communities, Hodges's critique of categorial models of community (centers versus margins, insider versus outsider), which focus on individualist notions of identity and becoming the other, led us to explore Probyn's analysis of community as surface and participation as occurring in communities of sense. Her analysis shifted the focus to a more relational model of community, which we had seen in Clarke's project at a women's center and in Deller's participatory projects. It enabled us to explore the ways in which some participatory and community artists create situations that support dialogue across boundaries and give participants the field.

The projects in chapters 3 and 4 speak to forms of participation through which ultimately the other as stranger becomes known as neighbor, friend, newcomer, or audience member. In our analysis so far, forms of dialogue, having a voice, having a say, having control over forms of discourse, register, and tone, have all been viewed through the idea of the other as someone known or someone to become known. A stranger is a friend you haven't made, someone who doesn't yet belong with you.

In this chapter, we want to develop an analysis of a fourth genre of participation, one in which the other is regularly encountered but may never become known. We do this through the concept of *publics*. Building on Dewey (1927), Warner (2002), Varnelis (2012), and others, we develop our analysis from the idea of relations between strangers. We shall put the concept of publics into play with notions of live encounter, voice, dialogue, and community in order to understand our last genre of participation: *participatory publics*.

As we have progressed through the book we have made small moves from done and dusted projects like StoryBank and Humanaquarium to include in our discussion projects in progress such as Anja's Spheres of Wellbeing and Rachel's Women's Centre project. In this chapter, we will further expand our horizons to include a consideration of people's everyday experiences of large-scale public technologies and we will conclude with a look at a project that is currently a proposal. This will enable us to explore how the conceptual tools we have developed in this book help us to create and articulate on our own technological imaginary of participatory digital publics.

On Publics

A few papers have been published in HCI recently that have used various conceptions of *publics* to help understand new domains of participation and collaboration. Le Dantec et al. (2012), for example, works with John Dewey's (1927) analysis in *Publics and Its Problems* to help conceptualize designs to support communication and collaboration in a women's refuge. Likewise, DiSalvo (2012) uses Dewey's analysis to explore more generally the role of design as a discipline in supporting public engagement in civic and political issues. Lindtner et al. (2011) use a different starting point, namely, Warner's (2002) analysis of media publics and counterpublics, to analyze the practices that emerged around a photo-sharing website, which they developed and deployed on a student campus. But what is a public? How does it differ from a community, an audience, or a network of family and friends?

A starting point for many accounts of publics is the distinction between *the* public and *a* public. Warner uses the term *the* public to refer to identifiable, countable totalities of people that form entities such as nations or states. The "Great British Public" is a term often used loosely, but essentially it is constituted, defined, and enumerable in some way, for example as any person who holds a British passport or any person who is eligible to vote in UK elections. There are many ways of categorizing people to define the public, for example, by ethnicity, religion, creed, or geography. The key point is that what unites these people is defined *in advance* and often by someone else.

In contrast, *a* public is *self-organizing* in that the association between people that constitute *a* public does not exist until it is brought into being by some common experience (Warner 2002). Warner, interested as he is in media, talks of a text (or other media content) being published and a public emerging around it. In a similar way, Dewey talks of a public coming into existence by virtue of experiencing the consequences of other people's actions. In any transaction, consequences arise. If only those who are party to the transaction feel the effects of those consequences, then the transaction is private. If others beyond those who are party to the transaction feel the effects, then the transaction is public, and a public arises in response to those consequences.

Although publics emerge in response to a shared experience, that sharing is not limited to a collection of people bounded in time or space (for example a theatre audience). Neither does it imply that the individuals are known to each other, as in some construals of community or family. For Warner and Dewey, a public is constituted primarily through relations between strangers:

[A public] unites strangers through participation alone, at least in theory. Strangers come into relationship by its means, though the resulting social relationship might be peculiarly indirect and unspecifiable. (Warner 2002, 75)

But because of their shared experience, the strangers of a public are not mysterious exotic creatures or aliens, nor are they strangers yet to become friends. We may never meet the other people making up a public. Yet we hear from them and see the trace of their actions through the texts in circulation, and we respond to them on the basis of this appearance. A public thus creates, as Arendt (1958) might say, a *space of appearance* through which strangers participate. But a public does not have to be exclusively made up of strangers. We may have friends and intimates, who are all members of a public with us, but that prior relation is not the basis for their participation in the public. So projects in the public sphere contrast with projects such as VJing, Personhood, and the Women's Centre projects, in which designers meet participants in person over periods of time forming personal relationships and sometimes even attachments. Projects in the public sphere also differ from the kinds of community projects we have described (Bespoke and StoryBank), in which participants are defined beforehand in terms of boundaries such as the geographical place and time where they live, belong, or work.

Although a public is made up of strangers, that does not mean they are simply a collection of individuals. A public is reflexive in the sense that the individuals who constitute it are aware of others who share a common experience. They may be "people like myself" or they may be people who are different from me in ways I can understand. This reflexivity is reinforced by the fact that a public is an active not passive space of appearance. A public is thus a very live entity, richly textured with friends, family, and strangers experiencing Dewey's consequences or Warner's texts in many different ways. They are aware of each other, able to form their own positions, to deliberate, to circulate their views and opinions, to respond in many different ways to the dialogue that builds up around the shared experiences they create.

At the time when Dewey and even Warner were offering their analyses of publics, the kinds of communication infrastructures that were available to support a public were very different to what they are now. The confluence of corporate broadcast media communications, the Internet, and personal communication media has created a powerful and deep platform for what we might think of as participatory networked publics. Similar to Rancière's emancipated spectator, the members of a public can participate simply by being there, they can talk among themselves from a diversity of perspectives, or they can talk back and from individual and collective views.

Rihanna in Concert: Making Performers of Us All

Recently, one of my (Pete's) daughters attended a pop concert in Manchester, United Kingdom. At home I saw her Facebook status update, designed no doubt to impress and amuse her Facebook friends: "Well bored ... just waiting for Rihanna to come on stage." Later my younger daughter, also at home, said she had received a phone call from her sister, who had been holding the phone aloft so that she could hear Rihanna live and the audience singing along and shouting. Later still, she received a photo and video.

This example captures much of the richness and complexity of a participatory public in play. The copresent audience extends the public to include people on the end of a phone call and people logged into Facebook. While Rihanna performs for her audience, texts and media are circulated by that audience, creating a larger nonpresent network of more-or-less friends and strangers. Even people outside the arena can hear the music as bystanders and they can buy merchandise as if they had been ticket holders. People hang around outside soaking up the somewhat secondhand experience of the buzz and confusion of the event. The audience, the crowd, the networked friends, family, and strangers all participate as part of a richly textured public. But the participative experience is different for these differently connected people. As audience member, the experience is one of taking part in a live performance, something that extends beyond passive consumption. Of course, there is some aspect of the experience, which is listening to a performance, but more important is the experience created by being physically part of an audience of twenty-one thousand other people of similar age and interests and even fashion sense as yourself, not only hearing and seeing the music but also feeling it in your chest, feeling the heat and excitement of the crowd, moving, jumping, bouncing, and surging with the beat.

Rihanna has so far sold more than twenty million albums and sixty million singles worldwide, and a significantly larger proportion of the planet's population will have heard her songs in bars and on the radio. They too are part of Rihanna's public, so simply being someone who knows or hears her songs is not that special. But buying a ticket and traveling a significant distance to take part in one of the live performances makes that participant special in terms of the statement it makes about him or her to others as someone who puts in that effort for Rihanna and special in terms of someone being witness to a specific event at a specific place and time. Other members of Rihanna's public may be watching it on TV, receiving video or audio on their phone from the members of the audience, may feel connected and may feel special, but that feeling is of a different order to that of those who were "there on the night."

The way Rihanna's public uses mobile phones to update status pages and upload photos or stream live audio or video is not about pirating her music; it is more about giving other people of significance to them a chance to share what's happening to them. It may also be a chance to show off. With a Facebook status update, they are potentially informing all Facebook users what is happening to them, but more significantly all of their Facebook friends and so this is a very public act. But in the case of sharing a photo or a video or audio recording taken at the event, this is more often about sharing that moment with a particular person, echoing again that idea of uniqueness. Part of the experience of participation is thus a play between intimate acts and public statements.

In chapter 5, we discussed Probyn's and Hodge's very different but related experiences of belonging in community. In a participatory public such as Rihanna's, the presence of multiple centers and multiple simultaneous positionings seems much closer to Probyn's analysis of belonging constituted by relationships of differentiation, creation, and innovation than to the communities of practice models critiqued by Hodges, implying as they do a trajectory from periphery to center. Participation for my daughter isn't just about consuming the spectacle, being positioned as audience or crowd or merchandise buyer. It is all of those perhaps, but it is simultaneously positioning herself as orator or commenter, creating her own audience, of me, her Facebook public, her sister, and her friends after the event, multiple positionings as producer and consumer of and in an experience. Probyn also talks of a periodicity in belonging, times of mutual invisibility alternating with visibility, and there is a temporality to this kind of public in which people come together briefly to participate intensely, to consume and to create, and then to dissipate but to remain a public in virtue of the shared experience, and on some occasions, for some time and some people, to let the dialogue go on beyond the event. The Rihanna experience then configures a new kind of emancipated spectator. It's not that the spectator participates by simply becoming the performer or responsively engaging with the performance on its own terms. Rather, they become their own kind of performer, curating and remediating the performance for their own audiences.

In chapter 3, we presented Bishop's analysis of the contrasting participatory aesthetics of Soviet and Western participatory art. Recall that she argued that for the CAG collective of Soviet Russia, compared with the *Happenings* of the United States, the aesthetic experience occurred in the dialogue after the event. In chapter 3, we argued that this distinction suggests that there are a number of potential temporal locations for participative experience. In the BOSOP project (chapter 4), participation is required for the event to happen at all. In Humanaquarium (chapter 3), participation is the point of the event and is contained within it. In the CAG aesthetic it occurs after the event. In the case of the Rihanna concert, event and dialogue about it occurs before, during, and after. My daughter updates her Facebook while waiting for the concert to start. She shares audio or video and sends texts and makes calls during and after. The aesthetics of participation extend the event in time and across space. There is a more complex openness to this genre of participation. In chapter 3, we described the openness of Humanaquarium and Open Burble as examples of events whose components are given but whose combination is open to participation. In these kinds of projects the authorial voice is strong. We contrasted them with the kinds of openness we see in participatory projects such as BOSOP and Personhood in chapter 4. In these projects, relationships are formed in order to determine what the project should be. This is a kind of openness in which the designer's voice is quieter. In participatory publics the relative position of author and participants is not the issue. The performance is clearly staged and the audience clearly completes it by being there and responding, but the staged performance is not the only center, not the only performance. The openness of this genre makes the author-performer subject and at the same time makes authors-performers of the audience, too.

The kind of openness experienced in participatory publics, an openness in which we are simultaneously audience and performer communicating to friends and strangers, individuals and groups, can create a participatory subjectivity in which you are never sure who can or will be able to see what. For example, similar to most people, my (Pete's) Facebook "friends" are a hybrid mixture of family, friends, colleagues, acquaintances, friends of friends (effectively strangers to me), and so on, all from very different parts of my life. But on Facebook the boundaries between these different groups becomes simultaneously permeable, opaque, and hard to police. On a recent family holiday trip I tried on silly hats outside a souvenir shop and pulled funny faces while my daughter took snaps. After the trip, I did not upload the photos onto my Facebook page, but my daughter uploaded one onto hers and tagged me. By doing so, she made it viewable by all my friends even though they were not her friends. I received several "likes" for the photo plus a comment from a member of the international HCI research community, "Really Peter, how will I be able to take you seriously again ☺." Although my colleague's response was humorous and ironic, it testifies to the complexities of this form of openness in which not only who gets to see what but also who gets to control who sees what is open. The boundaries between what is private and what is public become hard to police and they become reconfigured whether one likes it or not.

Strictly Come Dancing: The Public Talk Back

If the Rihanna example reveals to us a new kind of emancipated spectator, one who actively engages by becoming a curator, performer, remediator, and recirculator of texts, then TV celebrity game shows such as *Strictly Come Dancing* (*Dancing with the Stars* in the United States) reveal to us a public in which members not only talk among themselves but also talk back.

As a participative experience, these shows have a number of interesting features, particularly in the age of networked participatory publics. In these shows, celebrities agree to take part in a competition (dancing or ice skating, for example). The celebrities have no significant prior experience of dancing; rather, the point is to learn how to dance ballroom or to dance on ice. To this end, each celebrity is teamed up with a world-class professional as a dance partner. The professional trains the celebrities and choreographs their dance routines, which are then performed live in front of a studio audience and professional judges, as well as the TV audience at home.

The fact that the people taking part as contestants are celebrities means they are already known to the viewing public; the public's curiosity is thus already piqued before the series begins—how will Edwina Curry (ex-member of parliament) or Robby Savage (ex-professional footballer) cope with the Argentine Tango? The interest then is in how they shape up in this new context and what this reveals about their "real" character beyond their celebrity persona. As audience to this experience, we are witness to an encounter with otherness.

In BBC TV's *Strictly Come Dancing*, a new dance is learned and performed each week. The TV audiences watch the show and hear the panel of expert judges give feedback and rate the performances of the teams. Regular viewers get to know the judges' quirks, blind spots, and general dispositions, and each judge plays into a particular style. It becomes possible to second-guess the judges' responses and even the scores they will give. After many years of family viewing, my (Pete's) own family is remarkably accurate at anticipating the judges' scores, usually within a mark for all judges, except for the occasional (and often shocking) surprise.

In addition to the main show, pressing the interactive red button on the TV controller enables viewers to hear a commentary over the dances during the broadcast. Commentaries are provided by different people each week but usually a professional dancer and another celebrity who has some previous connection to the program. This provides another layer of commentary on the performance, often advising on technical problems or inside information on what's happening or anticipating the judges' scores. Another layer of commentary, this time by the public themselves, is available through the many blogs dedicated to the event, BBC official blogs and others. The BBC blog (BBC 2011) contains comments from watchers about the general features of the show and about the voting:

3. At 23:27 15th Oct 2011, Fannichanel wrote:
I think the judges are more in sync with the viewers this series ... either that or I'm getting better at judging !! Really enjoying the shows this year definitely the best series so far x

7. At 08:08 16th Oct 2011, waltzingjenny wrote:
Robbie and Ola did really well I am glad he is getting better. Chelsee and Pasha were underscored slightly I think, she did her cha cha really well and they are a great team, Jason and Christina were overscored a bit, it was a brilliant dance but he needs to work on posture and footwork. I loved the Broadway theme, hope there are more theme nights, it really adds to the show!!

8. At 10:00 16th Oct 2011, MrsArcanum wrote:
Definitely get the feeling both Len & Bruno are judging the same as the do for *Dancing with the Stars* where limited dance style content is allowed provided it is a show stopper. Len of the purist days of last year has disappeared.

In addition to these many sources of information, comment and opinion is available to the public before, during, and after the event. In the early days of the program, but less so now, my children would sit on the sofa watching "Strictly" while texting or Facebooking their friends about the scores and their thoughts about the performance, costumes, music, and so on, creating an extended public whose members may not even be watching the program, a live running commentary on a live televised event.

In between the weekly live shows the dialogue continues. In addition to gossip and reviews in the popular press, there is a daily TV show that reviews the previous weekend's show and anticipates the next, seeking views and comments from the celebrities, the judges, previous celebrities, and so on. Videos from the training studios reporting on each remaining contestant's progress as he or she learns the next week's routine are also shown. If one does miss the live event or the results show, there are often references to last week's performance in these commentaries, and there is thus a feeling that one needs to catch up and keep up. Indeed, watching a recording of the show in order to catch up before the next week is still a regular pastime in my house.

The live performance show, the weekday gossip programs, the blogs, the red button, the daily press, texting friends from the sofa—all of these participatory mechanisms provide a rich tapestry by which a public can participate, form opinions, and have a say in outcomes. But they have their most direct say over outcomes through voting each week on which contestants they would like to see go through to next week's show. This voting itself is designed as a kind of formal dialogue. The public gets to see the judges' scores before they themselves vote and can thus vote in response to the judges' rankings. The judges' scores and public votes are combined so that all parties can see what the effect the public vote has been. This decides which two couples have to dance again: the dance off. But, in the weekly dance off, only the judges' votes count and they decide who leaves the competition. This pattern repeats itself each week until the final. But in the final, although the judges still comment and score the contestants and thus influence public opinion indirectly, their scores no longer count and the outcome is decided by the public votes alone.

A complex dialogical dynamic of control over outcomes between the public and the judges is played out at different time scales through the mechanism of voting. The public finds out how the rankings lie after the judges' scores and they then have a chance to respond to change those rankings. Ultimately, the judges decide who goes out but the public decides who the judges decide between. In the long game, the public only have to ensure that their favorite couples get to the final where only their vote counts, and to do that they have to keep their favorites out of the bottom two, where their vote doesn't count.

Voting becomes the means by which members of the public can express their opinions and views and seek to change the course of the show from that determined by the judges (and vice versa). Much dialogue and comment centers on the judges' scoring of the dance. One of the recurring discussions is that although the judges purportedly score on the basis of technique, performance, and storytelling, it is often thought that the public vote on the basis of celebrity status and comic value. Certainly each week brings surprises as, for example, when a pair scored highest by the judges ends up in the bottom two after public voting, and vice versa. But such undesired outcomes one week can lead to increased voting the next week in order to avoid similar catastrophes.

In "Strictly," voting, seeing the outcomes, commenting via blogs, getting the backstory via newspapers, the red button, and the weekday update shows are all part of the participative experience that is highly dialogical. Of course, many people watch "Strictly" and never vote, many people vote and never go on the blogs, many people never watch the weekday updates. But this does not mean that they are in some sense more peripheral participants; rather, we see multiple positions from which people connect through multiple models of participation, all of which mutually influence one another.

The richly textured ecology of participation through which members of the public consume and contribute a multivoiced and multicentered participative experience creates a dynamic narrative that has its own liveness to which the public must pay attention in order to participate. Through this ecology, the public participates in what Warner refers to as poetic world making, and shows such as "Strictly" illustrate the complex layering of such poetic worlds. The show itself, of course, creates a complex poetic of music, movement, and narrative, but the public creates ever more complex layers of action and narrative that intersect and interact with the live TV performance. However, the liveness is also multidimensional with different temporal granularities layered within one another and up against one another—the time span of the live show, the window of opportunity for voting, the wait until the results show, the blogs and review programs, people texting one another during and after the event, anticipating what will happen next, reflecting on what has happened, and offering opinions on what should and shouldn't happen, the buildup to the final over the three months. There are also multiple centers, the red button channel, the post-series tour, the blogs, the voting, and the press. The voices are multiple, reflecting multiple opinions, from multiple points of view, sometimes conflicting sometimes consonant. Shock and horror and much discussion and dissent when the public vote puts the judges' top-rated pair in the results-show dance-off. But the "Strictly" production team is also in their turn responsive to the public mood as picked up through these multiple channels and through the press. They respond, for example, in the live show and the daily reviews to the emerging gossip about the celebrities, to public concerns that a certain celebrity might have unfair advantage because of dance training as a child, and even to the fact that a judge's idiosyncratic gesture or expression is becoming annoying.

The participative experience in these media events has a liveness that is beyond any simple definition of openness such as a *work in movement*, in which the media authors have a strong control over content but the public has control over outcomes although they do not speak with a single voice. The relationships are dialogical, emergent, reflexive, and self-organizing, and poetic worlds are created beyond and around the event. There is certainly an experience of dipping in and dipping out but there is also a sense of things going on without you when you have dipped out. For Warner, publics are constituted through the emergence of these multiple centers and multiple voices resulting in what he terms the reflexive circulation of texts:

No single text can create a public. Nor can a single voice, a single genre, even a single medium. All are insufficient to create the kind of reflexivity that we call a public, since a public is understood to be an ongoing space of encounter for discourse. Not texts themselves create publics, but the concatenation of texts through time. Only when previously existing discourse can be supposed, and when a responding discourse can be postulated, can a text address a public. (Warner 2002, 90)

A public then is a place of encounter and dialogue. This entails a self-referentiality, a cumulative experience, intertextuality, and intersubjectivity, and a persistence beyond a single discourse or text. A text (or utterance) is built on and responds to those that have gone before or will come later. These texts take many forms including, in the case of "Strictly," blog posts, votes, and televised conversations, all reflexively circulated among strangers. These utterances of different individuals, different voices, are put into circulation among strangers, with the authors having little control over either their journey or their final destination. This is a kind of openness to public participation that is both liberating and dangerous, as Warner (2002) points out:

When appearing in a public field, genres of argument and polemic must accommodate themselves to the special conditions of public address; the agnostic interlocutor is coupled with passive interlocutors, known enemies with different strangers, parties present to a dialogue situation with parties whose textual location might be in other genres or scenes of circulation entirely. The meaning of any utterance depends on what is known and anticipated from all of these different quarters. (89–90)

Having a Vote and Having a Voice

The participatory and dialogical experience of voting in celebrity TV shows such as "Strictly" contrasts strongly with many people's experiences of civic participation and especially political elections. Many countries consider the level of participation in elections an important index of the health of their democracies. For example, persistently low public turnout for general elections is often read as indicating the public's disaffection with the political process. Following a low turnout, newspapers tend to discuss publics' disenchantment with a process that seems to them to change the country's management but not the substance of its polity. There is a sense in these circumstances that people feel that voting does not enable them to exercise their voice in the way that they want. Whereas they may want a significant change of political direction for their country, they may find themselves faced with a choice between two or three major parties that hardly differ from each other. Furthermore, many of these political parties may also seem bland and managerial, unresponsive to the needs and desires of the electorate. In such circumstances, not voting may be the most eloquent expression of one's wishes and an appropriately crafted response to party blandness and irrelevance that citizens have available to them. And so voting loses its credibility as an effective form of engagement.

Even when political voting is experienced as effecting political change, it is seen by many as an insufficient form of participation in the country's decision making. It is an infrequent utterance—once every four or five years and it is a fairly one-dimensional utterance—this candidate or that. Civic participation requires ongoing involvement, a sense of effecting change and belonging to a process, not just an occasional vote. Attending town hall meetings, consulting with local representatives, and engaging with civic organizations exemplify the traditional ways in which people have ongoing involvement with the political process. For some, the Internet and Twitter have become important supports for their civic engagement by providing a means by which people with shared interests and values can communicate with each other and act collectively.

A number of HCI projects have considered the potential of digital media to provide members of the public with a voice without the time investment required of more traditional forms of civic engagement, such as town hall meetings. As part of the Bespoke project to contribute to innovation, inclusion, and development in Callon and Fishwick, an underresourced area in the north of England, a voting device called Viewpoint was implemented to open up lightweight and ongoing methods of participation in public deliberation and decision making (Taylor et al. 2012). During a trial period, local organizations and elected officials were allowed to post questions on Viewpoint devices that were located in public spaces in the area. Members of the public could then vote using the voting devices or post a text message in response.

Before Viewpoint was developed, the design team explored their design concept and issues of civic participation surrounding it with members of the public. People's opinions on traditional forms of consultation and participation were fairly negative. According to Taylor et al. (2012), "residents generally felt that their input had no effect and their voices were ignored" (1364). Residents were regularly consulted on local issues, but they rarely saw any action taken as a result and reported feeling consultation fatigue and disillusionment as a consequence. At the same time, public representatives reported difficulty getting good quality feedback in their consultation exercises with the residents. When commenting on the design concept, residents were generally positive and suggested placing it in shops and community centers. Of more relevance to our interest in understanding the potential of voting to give a voice, residents and representatives agreed that action had to follow from these polls. One housing association representative stated that it would be silly to put questions on without knowing what could be done once residents had responded to them. Both residents and representative were keen to have a system that would enable votes to change things in the community and to change people's understanding of the community. They both see value in voting as long as it is dialogical and as long as questioning and voting are responsive acts, attuned to the potential of the other to act in response to them.

The votes and responses from the originator of the poll were made publicly available. Over a two-month period, eight weekly questions were posted and nearly 1,800 votes were cast. The action that followed the polls ranged, for example, from placing a dumpster in the community, making a formal request for extra resources to tackle dog fouling, and making contact details available for people who were interested in community improvement activities. Whether residents would consider actions such as these to be responsive to, or shaped by, their vote is not clear. It is likely that for some at least, providing the skip would be seen as a direct response. It is the kind of responsive practical action that was also encouraged in the BOSOP project and that resulted in the participants rewriting the appointment letter and redesigning the traffic flow in parts of the hospital grounds. They are practical responses shaped by ongoing dialogue, actions that can relatively quickly make the kind of material difference that patients and staff identified as important. By contrast, the kind of response that prioritizes funding for dealing with dog fouling may be seen as a brush off, reminiscent of national political discourses in which priorities and promises are made but not always acted on. Similarly, simply providing the contact details of people interested in community volunteering may be seen as a token response, because such details could have been posted in the community center before any consultation. Actually gathering together a group of interested volunteers and organizing a program of work might have been a more authentic response.

Politicians and commentators often talk about voting and opinion polling as giving people a say. We have already argued in chapter 5 that "having a say" does not constitute dialogue. By contrast, having a voice means being able to act in ways that create new understandings and open up new possibilities for action. Voting could be seen as giving people a voice if a person's vote could be seen as responsive and responded to. But more often voting and opinion polling limits one's sense of agency, not simply because there is no response to the vote but also because the voting mechanisms are not designed to allow the complex and textured nature of the dialogues that underlie them to be made visible.

Hauser (1999) attacks political opinion polling as a technological incursion into the liveness of public deliberation that does not connect with vernacular rhetoric and that derails the process of opinion formation in vernacular publics. He argues that the methodology of the opinion survey assumes that random members of the general populace can be substituted for actively, dialogically engaged voices of a vernacular public, assuming that anyone can be interrogated on a particular topic *salve veritate*, because everyone is omni-opinionated. It assumes that all opinions carry equal weight (irrespective of the personal histories and experiences of those taking part), and it takes control over what questions get asked apart from those required to answer them, assuming also that all questions are equally relevant to all participants. As Hauser puts it, "survey research transmutes public opinion from a discursive phenomenon to be interpreted and studied critically, into a behavioral phenomenon to be quantified and studied scientifically" (191).

Hauser also points out that there is a dialogical irony and conceit at the heart of survey research methodology. Although premised on the superior ideology of objective scientific enquiry, there is an inevitably political relationship between survey researcher and participant. As Hauser puts it, they are "an intensely political mode of discourse" (193). In order to obtain a "truthful" measure from the respondent they are questioning, they disguise the true intent behind the question and do not reveal how the answer will be used in order to disguise what it is that the survey commissioner is seeking to learn. In the hands of powerful political elites, analysis of participants' "naive" responses is taken as evidence for a unified public opinion in favor of, or in opposition to, such and such an issue without the participant having ever been informed about what they were "giving evidence"' about. Instead, Hauser argues for a return to focus on listening to the vernacular voices of the public and focusing our attention on the dialogue that constitutes the process of opinion formation.

Vernacular Voices and Social Media

Vernacular rhetoric is the term Hauser uses to refer to the discourses that constitute the public deliberation and opinion formation of ordinary people. Following Bakhtin, he draws our attention to a contrast among the official rhetorics of politicians, media, and empowered elites and the dissensual voices of the public. Vernacular rhetoric is the place to find the active deliberative, reflexive voices of opinion formation based on people making sense of the consequences of an utterance on their own and others' lives.

Vernacular "talk" is essential for a societal conversation to ensue, since conversation presupposes shared meanings among dialogic partners able to test each other's claims and find evidence from their own experiences and knowledge to evaluate the relevance of these claims to their lives. (Hauser 1999, 10)

Hauser's analysis of vernacular publics reinforces Suchman's arguments from chapter 4 that forms of engagement with rhetorical publics need to respond to the lived experience of people and "require[s] an autobiography, a presence, and a projected future" (Suchman 2007, 23). In chapter 5, we discussed the Women's Centre project in the context of Deller's participatory art, arguing that an important motivation for Rachel Clarke and Jeremy Deller is starting conversations, but how is this done and what form do these conversations take, when people are not living and working together, do not know each other, and when their encounters are distributed across time and place? In our Rihanna and *Strictly Come Dancing* examples, we saw how vernacular discourses emerge among publics around media events and how, in the case of "Strictly," voting can be a natural expression of opinions formed through such dialogue. But in describing these examples, we have not yet explored in detail the character and potential of these vernacular exchanges. Hauser is keen to show how vernacular rhetoric takes place in many spaces other than face-to-face encounters in coffee houses and bars. Film, theatre, literature, the TV, and news media all provided spaces for the expression of vernacular rhetoric. But Hauser wrote *Vernacular Voices* in 1999 and since that time, the emergence of social media has created new spaces of encounter and new opportunities for vernacular dialogue.

On September 20, 2011, one of us (Pete) happened to visit YouTube and one of the featured uploads was a video of Paul Simon singing "Sounds of Silence" as part of the tenth anniversary of the September 11 terrorist attacks in the United States. The video provoked the usual series of comments variously about Paul Simon's performance and a jokey account of how long it took him to write the song, and so on, but in addition it provoked a discussion about US foreign policy and the war in Afghanistan and Iraq. Here is an edited excerpt from a comment thread associated with a YouTube video (https://www.youtube.com/all_comments?v=3np0DMxXKzM):

95zoekirk95

R.I.P the 2976 Americans who lost their lives, but does anyone spare a thought for the 48644 innocent Afghans and 1690903 innocent Iraqis who have paid the price for this? Extremists take everything to the extreme, I just wish that the American population would know this and think before generalizing all the rest of the Muslim population, after all innocent Muslims were in those towers to.

95zoekirk95 1 day ago 8
The real victims of 9/11 are the innocent 1.5+ million Iraqi and Afghan civilians who were caught up in a ILLEGAL war !

Bugz904 1 day ago 5
@Bugz904
Agreed
As well as the present and future generations of Americans who have lost precious freedoms and stability here at home

jocarbart 50 minutes ago
@dugham94
I didnt really use the number millions.
What we are doing is just further destabilizing, despite the constant use of the term "nation building".
Logistically America would not be so deep down the rabbit hole of its own demise if we would just leave well enough alone and stop trying to police the world.
Nothing we have done has made a positive difference neither for our country nor those we occupy.
Just a waste of time. money, life, and resources.

jocarbart 52 minutes ago
Absolutely beautiful !!

deadmo62 2 hours ago
@95zoekirk95 - you do realize it wasn't 2976 Americans but rather 2976 people of all nationalities from around the world?

open6l 3 hours ago
@NicaraguaHD: because honoring and respecting the dead means remembering them. by remembering what happened, and by remembering and celebrating the lives of our loved ones who died, we are honoring their memory. no one is remembering this event because they think it will change the past; we are remembering to change the future. if you forget what happens, the past will repeat. for people like me who did lose people that day, it is important to us to look back and reflect.

This selection of comments about the Paul Simon performance seems to us to capture the kind of vernacular rhetorical public sphere that Hauser speaks of. The exchanges, similar to those on many other sites, are frank, sometimes rude, and confrontational, but they seem to involve concerned people expressing political and ethical opinions that are important to them.

Lim and Kann (2008) offer examples of how social media such as You-Tube can support something more such as public consultation including, in

2007, the teaming up of CNN and YouTube to support citizen participation in Democratic and Republican debates. Citizens submitted questions to candidates through videos, which they produced and uploaded, and were then presented on TV, to which the politicians responded. The result was a mix of engaging media entertainment and political debate.

During the democratic debate, a snowman asked candidates about his future in a world of global warming, a lesbian couple challenged candidates to answer whether or not they would be able to get married, and a man holding a gun which he called his baby inquired into candidates' positions on gun control. (Lim and Kann 2008, 77)

But although such events illustrate the extent to which social media has become part of mainstream politics, from the point of view of dialogical engagement, they use only a very limited part of the potential of the Internet. For sure, citizens get to have their unique voices heard and, more than this, video format provides them with the opportunity to exploit the space of appearance to rhetorical effect, but Lim and Kann argue that the citizen contribution is reduced to supplying a potentially comical point of departure for delegates' political point scoring. "Business as usual," they conclude. The public may have had a *say* but not a *voice* in that particular mediation of the networked public. Lim and Kann go on to describe more dialogical manifestations. "Listening to the City" (LTC) for example, engaged thousands of US citizens in online and offline meetings and discussions about how to rebuild the site and to create a memorial for the victims of the World Trade Center attacks of September 11.

The LTC final report outlines this monumental public deliberation "designed to give people a voice in re-building the World Trade Center site" (Civic Alliance 2002, 2). Around 4,500 participated in two, one-day town hall meetings, people who had never met before including "relatives of victims, downtown residents, survivors of September 11, emergency workers, business leaders, the unemployed and underemployed, interested citizens and community advocates" (Civic Alliance 2002, 2). This public was presented with six preliminary concepts and asked to comment, deliberate, and discuss. These two physical meetings were followed by an online consultation aimed at making it possible for "a broad cross-section of the region to help set priorities for rebuilding downtown New York and the surrounding area" (Civic Alliance 2002, 18). The online consultation reached an additional 818 citizens and the event lasted two weeks. These participants followed an agenda similar to the one that was followed in the town hall meetings, but the final report argues that the extended time available enabled a more detailed discussion. Indeed the report indicates that, "approximately 10,000 messages were exchanged during the online dialogue and important themes were sifted from it. Participants were able to make their priorities known through 32 polls based primarily on the themes that emerged from discussions" (Civic Alliance 2002, 18).

Both the town hall meetings and the online dialogues were carefully managed technological events. In the town hall, participants worked in round table groups of ten to twelve people with a facilitator. Networked laptops were used to record ideas generated during the discussions. Each table's input was transmitted to a coordinating team that identified the strongest contacts from the discussions and reported them back to all participants. This team also developed questions and priorities that were posted on large screens enabling all participants to compare their individual and group thinking to the larger collective. As indicated, polls were developed from the ground up to assist in people refining their views and moving the conversation on.

The online event did not run in parallel with the live events; rather, it occurred over two weeks, shortly after the town hall meetings, but it followed a similarly curated format. Participants were divided into about thirty discussion groups. Individuals' assignment to groups was done by computer and based on demographics and personal histories in order to ensure diversity of viewpoints.

Unlike typical Internet "chat" sessions, the online dialogue encouraged considered exchanges because participants did not have to be online simultaneously or respond immediately. Participants could read messages posted by members of their group and respond at their convenience. They could also follow the discussions underway in other groups and review a wide range of maps, letters from officials and other background documents that were made available online. (Civic Alliance 2002, 18)

The small-group format encouraged people to develop relationships, and working over an extended period with people who had different perspectives encouraged fresh thinking both individually and collectively. Evaluations of the process suggest that the experience of participation was meaningful and had an effect. One participant reported, for example,

"It was quite wonderful to exchange opinions with diverse people. I have to say it changed my perspective of democracy," said one participant. Said another, "[it was] fascinating to see that 5,000 people are able to communicate." And yet another said: "It was great to interact with others and bounce ideas [around], especially since we were from different backgrounds and demographics." (Civic Alliance 2002, 20) and Pete Hamill of the *New York Daily News* reported,

All around this vast room, you heard citizens saying politely to others, "What do you think?" and then listening—actually listening—to the replies. In this room "I" had turned to "we" ... and it was absolutely thrilling. (Civic Alliance 2002, 20)

In the online and offline discussions, the six design concepts received careful and critical consideration and, ultimately, were not well received. According to the final report, the public criticized them as "too dense, too dull and too commercial" (Civic Alliance 2002, 92):

"Listening to the City" had a direct and swift impact on the fate of these concept plans. Just weeks after the six plans were introduced as a starting point for discussion, the program they were based upon was set aside, largely because of sharp criticism at "Listening to the City" and other public feedback. (Civic Alliance 2002, 11)

LTC is in many ways an example par excellence of participatory publics. Over five thousand people were given a chance to meet and to exchange views and express their opinions on matters of direct consequence to their lives using a variety of traditional and networked technologies, and some, at least, came away with a feeling that they had taken part in something that made a difference on a grand scale. As was the case in the Viewpoint project, but on a more massive scale here, there is a sense in which people seemed to have come to a view and expressed opinion in the justified hope that something would be done, that their voice would make a difference, and for many it did. More than this, though, many participants seemed to have been personally transformed by the participative experience.

Were one to look more critically perhaps (without denying the undoubted success of this project, in its own terms), one might see this project as a participative experience that was carefully managed along the kinds of technological and rationalistic lines that Hauser fights against in his analysis of vernacular publics. Participants are carefully selected and grouped to be representative and to be diverse; questions and issues are carefully controlled, filtered, and made public by professional facilitators and "skilled staff"; and the process of interpretation of discussions and discourses is carefully controlled. Although opinions were polled based on themes that the facilitators identified from discussions, ultimately consensus was arrived at through voting. In the final report, one participant's view on the limitations of this method of aggregations and consensus formation is presented:

Some of the "voting" questions limited our ability to provide expansive answers, but I'm not sure how it could be different with so many people. (Civic Alliance 2002, 20)

If Lim and Kann's comment "business as usual" sums up the problem of having a voice but not being listened to, then this participant's comment sums up perfectly the problem of creating a mechanism that is expressive enough to capture that voice. Voting in its orientation toward creating consensus tends to hide the diversity that is present in the voices it seeks to express.

Considering LTC online in particular, Lim and Kann argue that perhaps it mimicked its offline analogue too closely without really harnessing the full potential of participatory media. Although LTC online gave people more time for deliberation, surprisingly the event engaged only 818 people compared with the 4,300 that attended the one-day town hall meetings. Perhaps the managed and formalized processes of consultation create something more like a Habermassian public sphere that frames dialogue as rational argument rather than vernacular rhetoric and provides little room to engage with the dissenting voices that we heard earlier in relation to the Paul Simon performance at the ten-year anniversary. But unlike the Paul Simon discussion, the LTC discussion was at least addressing someone and creating a response.

All of this pessimism about digital democracy occurs at a time when millions of people participate on YouTube, TV game shows, eBay, and Facebook. There is hardly a citizen who would not have at least heard of, if not participated in them, at some level. When we look back at our examples of Rihanna and "Strictly," it would seem that the power of social media should be precisely the power to harness vernacular voices of a networked public and to create digital public spaces for democratic decision making and opinion formation on a massive scale. That is not to say that digital public space for civic engagement should be more like *Strictly Come Dancing* (although it is a tempting thought). Rather, the question is whether it is possible to imagine a platform that could provide the conditions necessary for vernacular publics to form, for individuals to share their experiences, to make arguments, and to come to opinions within a space of appearance that supports and valorizes diversity and interdependence. But what are the necessary conditions? Hauser presents five criteria for the emergence of a vernacular public that we interpret in the following in terms of their relevance as a starting point for imagining such a form of digital civic engagement.

Permeable Boundaries   Publics are multiply centered and multiply voiced, comprising individuals, individuals in collectives, subpublics and counterpublics, more active members, and more peripheral members, outspoken

minorities, and silent majorities. This diversity is essential to their deliberative purpose. A discussion between a group *in public* is usually a discussion
half-oriented to that public, and the public will draw inferences about the
group based on their reading of that discussion. Such inferences may not
be the ones intended by those having the discussion. Hence, it is important
to be able to control the boundaries of subgroups within a public, when,
for example, the group seeks to come to a common view uninfluenced by
members of the public about issues that are nevertheless of public interest. But these boundaries need to be permeable, controllable, and visible,
and there needs to be an ethics of boundary crossing as well as an ethics of
dialogue within a boundary. As with Probyn's communities, we need to be
able to alternate easily between being in private, being in public, and being
in private-in-public.

Activity   Publics must be actively engaged in dialogue and there must be
multiple perspectives in play. People should be treated as differently placed
equals with views on a common issue. Opinions must be formed through
dialogue and individuals must be open to change. People must feel that
what they have to say, their opinions, and their experiences are listened to
and make a difference to outcomes.

Contextual Language   Public deliberation must be anchored in personal and
collective experience, yet such experience is often expressed through differently contextualized vernacular languages. Hauser argues that institutional
powers and epistemic elites often undermine the acceptability of vernacular
language within a public sphere. As we saw in the BOSOP project described
in chapter 5, a discursive arena has to be designed such that individuals (in
that case nurses and patients) feel able to speak, have their voice heard, and
their experience acknowledged.

Believable Appearance   A public sphere is a space of appearance among
strangers. Individuals and collectives have images within that space of
appearance, which are collectively constructed. An important characteristic of public sphere is how and to whom it makes the space of appearance
sensible. Furthermore, the collective construction of appearance must be
done in a way that is believable and credible. How the space is designed
affects how believability, credibility, and authority are jointly constructed
and contested.

Tolerance   A rhetorical public sphere is composed of multiple centers and
multiple voices. Divergent perspectives, despite a willingness to change
and grow, make consensus not only difficult but unhelpful. Consensus can
be forced by dominant ideology and language neutralizing other voices or
by pandering to vested interests whose satisfaction is not in the general

interest. The rhetorical norm of a public sphere is a solution that "interdependent partners regard as acceptable for their own reasons" (Hauser 1999, 79).

Although Hauser sees his criteria as "criteria by which the defining conditions of any specific public may be gauged and criticised" (77), in the final section of this chapter we will try to use them as the starting point for imagining the design space for a digital civics platform that we are beginning to realize through two projects at Newcastle, the Social Inclusion through the Digital Economy Research (SiDE) Hub and the Mobility and Place (MyPlace) project.

A Technological Imaginary of a Digital Civics Platform

Within the United Kingdom there has been an increasing demand for research that delivers impact (social, economic, as well as academic) and that involves the public through participation in research. Within user-centered design, of course, involving members of the public as users and as codesigners is standard practice but, in addition, projects respond to this call by involving members of the public in steering committees and other governance structures as well as in town hall meetings to disseminate results of academic research. The aim of the SiDE project is to explore ways in which people at risk of social exclusion can be given better access to the potentially life-changing benefits of digital technologies platforms and services. One of the highlighted features of Newcastle's SiDE proposal was the formation of a one-thousand-strong user panel. Panel members receive newsletters, take part in surveys, attend research showcases, and take part as subjects in the evaluation studies of new technologies. But this framing of the panel has at times been problematic in terms of participation. Expressed quite simply, it is hard for a single academic research project to generate enough surveys, user requirement tasks, user testing studies, or participatory design workshops to convincingly engage more than one thousand members of the public. More recent discussion in the project has begun to reframe this public as "intellectual capital," people whose experiences can be put to use in framing, deliberating, and conducting research. The MyPLACE project aims to develop and test a digital platform that will enable members of the public to engage with local councils in the research, planning, and design of the urban environment. In this project citizens will be invited to take part as coresearchers and codesigners. But how can such levels of participation occur at the scale of more than a thousand people, short of unfeasibly expensive types of encounter such as "Listening to the City"? How can we build a participatory platform that would motivate members of the user panel to engage at scale deliberatively with the project, support the emergence of grassroots issues and vernacular rhetorics, but without becoming the undirected conversations of YouTube? How can we reconfigure the relationship between the panel and the project such that it becomes a vernacular voice in a real dialogue?

Designing a Participatory Platform

Hauser's normative criteria for a vernacular public described above provide a basis for thinking about the experience-centered design of the participatory platform. How might the normative criterion of *permeable boundaries* help to constrain decisions about anonymity and the management of public-private boundaries and the reflexivity of mutual action? How might the normative criteria of *contextual language* affect decisions about allowing people free expression in online public fora, and how does this relate to goals of validating individual experience? How does the criterion of *believable appearance* affect decisions about anonymity, traceability of actions, visibility of histories and biographies, and how does this conflict with permeability?

Forming a Public

Across the SIDE user panel there is a diverse range of skills including retired academics, schoolteachers, social workers, caretakers, and homemakers. This diversity offers a potential capital of expertise and viewpoints. As Nina Simon (2010) points out in her analysis of YouTube, social media provide an ecology of mechanisms for participation from simply browsing and having your data captured for a recommender system, through voting, commenting, and curating other's content, to creating one's own content (e.g., YouTube videos). We would thus expect some participants to be heavily involved as coresearchers on projects supported by the participatory platform. They would attend events and provide content, evidence, and data supported by a core team of paid researchers. Others would be engaged only with live workshops. Others still would be present online during such workshops to serve as critics and commentators and to vote online. Others still could collect output linking thematic issues for consideration.

Members of the user panel might be actively subscribed to the participatory platform and members of the general public would also have some access to events and output and be able to comment and vote and subscribe in order to take more active roles. We begin to imagine then, a reticulate sphere comprising professional project members acting as facilitators and managers and ambassadors, supporting members of the user panel, with varying levels of participation, working in the context of a general public. But in addition, subpublics based on shared interests and a shared viewpoint in the issues under discussion would also be supported. Furthermore, on a project-by-project basis, participants would be helped to identify and engage other bodies and institutions, such as local councils and third-sector organizations.

Beginning with Experience

As we saw with projects such as BOSOP, the Women's Centre, and Story-Bank, a good place to begin to understand issues and consequences is personal stories. Stories can be told in many ways—spoken, written, captured in photographs and videos—and many things are natural catalysts for stories, places, objects, events. People not only accrue but also constitute stories. Personal stories create a vernacular space in which everyone is an expert in their own experience, they can be used to connect people in a space of appearance in ways that connect to autobiographies, and they can serve to validate individuals and support a process of understanding issues from another's perspective.

Stories can be shared with others, and in so doing, can be used to stimulate new stories from others, stories that might support, contradict, extend, or complement. As we saw in the women's center, when stories are put into circulation, when they are made public, when they are shared across boundaries in a reticulate public sphere, they have the potential (sometimes positive, sometimes negative) to become something else, to take on new meanings. They can become evidence, they can become testimony, or they can become data, for example. The use to which stories are put is something that has to be managed within the platform.

It is possible that stories could accumulate virally. Provided that the means of recording them was widely available and easily accessible, core project members might submit stories through carefully managed events (as in BOSOP) but if these were made available online, more members of the public could add their own stories as well as comment and vote on others'. Sharing a story might even be a requirement for gaining access to the platform. But such storytelling would need to be curated, because unmanaged contributions can be irrelevant, unproductive, or simply offensive.

Stories are only one way in which to ground deliberation in vernacular experience. Stories are usually reconstructions after the fact. But how might the ecology of mobile and ubiquitous sensing technologies be used to capture live experience? We can imagine, for example, how in some projects concerned with the difficulties of disabled access in the city, that disabled and more able members of the public would be invited to undertake journeys together, to and through the city with location-aware devices. Participants might also carry mobile apps that enable them to photograph and otherwise record situations that were particularly good or bad parts of the journey experience and maybe vote on likes and dislikes. They might also record their dialogue as they proceed through the city or they may have a sampling device that enables participants to record only selected aspects of the journey. Such journeys would be plotted on maps and other representations of the city and commenting and voting used to annotate the maps. In other areas of the city, Viewpoint-style voting boxes might be used to capture the votes of passersby who may not even be part of the project. Boxes would be located in parts of the city that had been identified by participants as worthy of further consideration and questions would be framed by participants to explore the issues arising.

Analyzing Experience and Identifying Issues

If the participatory platform were a place for aggregating, viewing, and analyzing all of these stories and experiences, they could be used as a resource for town hall meetings to stimulate discussion, deliberation, and opinion formation much as in BOSOP. Colocated or online participants could be formed into small diverse groups as in "Listening to the City," and facilitators and experts could be used to identify emerging themes, which are relayed to other groups. But more than this, what if those debates were recorded live on video and streamed to the Internet where the public could vote and comment on emerging issues. Or, perhaps instead, group members (collectively or individually) when they arrive at a point for which they judge to be of significance, they could press a button to stream only the last thirty seconds of their discussions. These participant-selected highlights could be relayed to the public at large for a vote or to specific experts for comment and response.

In chapter 4, we talked about Asher's experiments in reconfiguring social arrangements in the art gallery, making the work of the gallerist visible to the visitors and contracting schoolchildren to design an exhibition in order to broaden participation. In "Listening to the City," participants discussed experiences and ideas in small groups, but trained facilitators and researchers identified themes in their discussions, which they interpreted and relayed to the larger group for comment and voting. But it is possible to imagine the participants themselves being enabled to carry out this process.

Crowdsourcing could be used to tag data online, identifying key words in texts that were transcribed online. Equipped with suitable technology for rapidly sifting, viewing, and editing video (see for example, Jackson et al. 2013), rather than experts and facilitators identifying themes and issues, participants themselves could be encouraged to explore the data and report back.

Finding Solutions and Going On

It is possible to envisage many possible uses for the participatory platform from coresearching people's experiences of the urban environment through supporting civic consultations and citizen juries to supporting large-scale participatory design. But for the purposes of illustration, consider the case of participatory design. It is possible to imagine participants running design competitions, engaging, for example, students from higher education institutions, providing them with video highlights to function as storyboards and scenarios to which they invite a design solution. Alternatively, imagine how potential design solutions might be envisioned by participants themselves. Design mockups, storyboards, or videos might be produced. These would be put online for comment, critique, and votes.

Networked Participatory Publics: A New Space of Potential

The networked participatory publics explored in this chapter have given us a way into a new kind of openness and a new space of potential and actual forms of social (re-)configuration. We characterized a public as an association between strangers that brings itself into existence in response to shared experiences. A public's response is the reflexive generation of dialogue and the construction of poetic worlds in relation to those shared experiences. The new form of openness is one in which an individual's participatory subjectivity is configured to have the potential to be simultaneously audience and performer, content consumer and producer, and center for the creation and transmission of remediated experiences. Whether it is a live gig or a TV show or a political debate, the character of a public in play is that of creating a shared experience, which is extended in time and space by those who take part.

The social (re-)configuration at issue speaks strongly to our analysis of Rancière's emancipated spectator in chapter 4. It is more than simply acknowledgment that an audience is actively engaged in the construction of meaning, and it is different than a requirement on the audience that they take part to complete the work. It is also more than simply arguing for

equality between performer and audience. It is a dialogical form of openness, in which differently placed individuals and collectives create and
consume.

We also noted a kind of liveness to publics in play. The experience is
of something that goes on without you. Burke, cited in Hauser (1999)
although written in 1973, perfectly captures this liveness:

Imagine that you enter a parlor. You come late. When you arrive, others have long
preceded you, and they are engaged in a heated discussion, a discussion too heated
for them to pause and to tell you exactly what it is about. In fact, the discussion had
already begun long before any of them got there, so that no one present is qualified
to retrace for you all the steps that had gone before. You listen for a while, until you
decide that you have caught the tenor of the argument; then you put in your oar.
Someone answers; you answer him, another comes to your defense; another aligns
himself against you, to either the embarrassment or gratification of your opponent,
depending on the quality of your ally's assistance. However the discussion is inter-
minable. The hour grows late, you must depart. And you do depart, with the discussion still vigorously in progress. (Burke 1973, 110–111)

In TV shows, such as *Strictly Come Dancing*, the experience of participation is in some sense similar to a *work in movement*. The show itself and
the participatory platform it relies on is carefully engineered. Although the
audience gets to vote on contestants, they don't get to choose who the
contestants are. But it is more than a work in movement. The participatory
platform creates the potential for multiple dialogues around the experience: the show itself, the daily reviews, the blogs, the popular press, and so
on. This rich texture of what Hauser refers to as vernacular dialogue potentially contributes to public opinion on who should win and who should
lose. Moreover, the audience has a control over these outcomes through
voting, but this is a control, which is shared in a dialogical way with the
judges, that leads to a complex dynamic control over outcomes that is distributed over time.

As we saw, Hauser critiques opinion polling as a very weak mechanism
for reconfiguration. Voting in elections, for example, is a layer of democratic
politics that seems not to reconfigure the political space at all and does not
change participant identity or subjectivity. It is a numerical process only,
which Rancière (2006) argues is not enough for democracy, which ought to
reconfigure the social, identity, subjectivity, and belonging. It does not do
this because it polices what is sensible. As we noted in chapter 4, for Rancière, modes of participation are determined by the modes of perception
that are available, and mode of perception—*the sensible*—refers to what is

visible, audible, sayable, thinkable, and doable. Political opinion polls and electoral votes leave what is visible, sayable, and doable under the control of those who call the vote or create the poll, and the space of what is sensible is usually limited from both sides. From the side of those who call the vote, the outcome of the vote provides little access to the complexly layered dialogues and deliberations that underpin it. From the side of those who vote, the options for action are determined elsewhere and have limited expressive power.

In a number of the projects we have discussed in this chapter, attempts have been made to embed decision making within a richer tapestry of participative dialogue. In Viewpoint, we saw how the project team, although deploying a lightweight voting mechanism, ensured that participation was seen as one in which what was being voted on was relevant to the vernacular dialogues that had taken place and also that the outcome of the polls would be acted on. The responsivity of the local council and other agencies created a minimal sense that the voting was part of a dialogue. "Listening to the City" created a dialogical space of discussions, shared experiences, stories, and voting on grassroots issue to empower those taking part. The diverse backgrounds of the participants and the carefully constructed dialogical space created was what Hauser would recognize as a vernacular dialogue and what Rancière would recognize as equality in difference. By making the diversity of experiences sensible, the social reconfiguration was possible, empowering ordinary citizens to require the planners, designers, and politicians to go back to the drawing board. Whereas the citizens could have simply been asked to vote on which of the planning concepts they preferred, instead they were empowered to create their own vision. Furthermore, because this process was visible to those in power, it had a moral authority that a simple vote could never have. Recall in chapter 4 we introduced Till's notion of *transformative participation* as reimagining of how professional knowledge is enacted in dialogue between professionals and the people who use their services. Till would have recognized "Negotiation of Hope" in "Listening to the City."

In our technological imaginary of a participatory platform we tried to make concrete one way in which designers might respond to the challenge of reconfiguring users in academic research projects, how they might reconfigure a "user pool" into an actively engaged citizenry. Although hopelessly underspecified, our aspiration was to open up a space for imagination and discussion and to crystalize what some of the defining characteristics of networked participatory public are.

The first is the ability to "sense" the public and for the public to sense each other—to be able to collect actions, experiences, and opinions of individuals. The second is to extend the reach of the sensible to actions, experiences, and opinions from individuals who are not colocated with the subject. The third is to be able to collect the utterances of large numbers of individuals and for those individuals to be able to see their own responses in relation to individuated others. The fourth is to support multiple ways in which individuals can make a contribution.

7 Dissensus, Design, and Participative Experience

Our main aim in writing this book was to develop a space for critical enquiry into participative experience. It grew out of one or both of us being involved with many of the projects that we have discussed and wondering what these projects were really about, why we were attracted to them, and what they might mean for HCI and for design. This work entails a critical dialogue with other approaches to participation in HCI, such as participatory design, in which we raise questions about how participation is configured (Vines et al. 2013). The core argument of the Vines et al. paper is that decisions made before and during participation, as well as how and by whom those decisions are made, affect heavily the quality of participants' involvement in design and their participative experience. We have continued this critical dialogue here by enquiring into the values, processes, and consequences of reconfiguring participation in more experimental participatory projects.

Experience has always been a core concept in our approach to HCI and design and, as HCI and design research has responded to social media, so participative experience has become central to our understanding of people's relations with technology. As we looked at and tried to make sense of participative experience, we were struck by its variety as it moved and changed and seemed always becoming in time and space.

The projects we have explored are generally works in process, never quite finished because there is no predetermined endpoint for them, never quite finalized because of their responsivity to the unpredictability of events. Many of them have an eventlike quality, and the experience of participating in a particular event is of making something unique happen. Intrinsically, the ineffability of events is the quality that gives them experienced value. However, as Dewey (1925) points out, when people recount experiences to each other, events become objects with meanings, serving the conversation or narrative and losing something of their ineffability,

immediacy, and uniqueness. Participatory projects strive to keep the experience alive in design in order to make sense of it. When we stand back a
little from individual projects to try to make sense of events, we connect
and compare them with each other and in so doing, run the risk of losing
their episodic quality, their uniqueness, and the primacy of their becoming.

The projects are particular kinds of events that depend on the contingent nature of their happening and the meaningfulness of their recounting.
They are experiments that try to figure participative experience and participant subjectivity by creating openings and following where they lead. People now tend to think of experiments in terms of the controlled procedures
of natural science. However, there is an older meaning that resonates with
the innovative character of participatory projects. It emphasizes developing practical knowledge by trying out new things, or even more generally,
learning from experience. Participatory projects try out new modes of participation to learn about their potential for enriching lived experience. In
the process they learn that participative experience is something that is and
may always be in a process of becoming, and they learn that participant
subjectivity is always plural, responsive, and situated.

Looking across individual projects and events, we see patterns of similarity and difference that illustrate different ways of creating dialogical space
in which the meaning of participation is performed through the communications and the relationships between participants. The seminal insight for
us came from critical reflection and reading about the most straightforward
of participatory projects, those in which audience members are invited to
become performers for a while. Rancière's The Emancipated Spectator opened
our eyes to the varieties of participation that occur in staged events beyond
the binary producer-consumer model that encourages playing around with
roles to encourage participation. Rancière's work indicated an alternative
dialogical approach based on making existing patterns of participation sensible. The notion of "inbetween" belonging was also generative, drawing
attention as it did to the experience of living between conventional categories of participation and identification. The generativity is in recognizing
the potential for creativity in between the commonsense world of roles
and expectations and the aspirational world of imagination and fantasy
or between self and other. The dialogic of "inbetween" belonging is not
in summing these different parts but in exploring together the potential
between them. In doing this, we render open the social configuration of
space and time, as Deller (2002, 2012) does in his "inbetween" work, for
example, when he brings the past into the present through reenactment.
Making participation sensible, exploring the potential space in-between,

giving participants the field as Deller does, can all evoke multilayered dissensual conversations that support fresh experiences of belonging in a space that is from another time.

We have learned in two different ways from engaging with the projects and with a strangely eclectic literature that helped us make sense of them. Cognizant of Gregory Bateson's (1973) categories of learning, it seems to us that, first, we have learned from the projects something about their potential to enrich experience by reconfiguring participation through design, and second, we have learned about learning in this context, or more precisely about enquiry and epistemology in HCI and design.

Reconfiguring Participation through Design

In chapter 4, we suggested that, when seen as a process of redistributing the sensible, design is concerned with what modes of perception and participation are made available through the production, reproduction, and transformation of sociomaterial assemblages. According to Rancière, the distribution of the sensible refers to a policed ordering of what can be thought, discussed, and imagined. The policed order is a consensual order that controls modes of participation by controlling modes of perception, that is, by making particular ways of seeing and thinking common sense and unquestionable. Rancière suggests that politics and art—the interdependence of policing and sensibility—makes the trick of consensual order sensible and ultimately impotent. In participatory projects, the production, reproduction, and transformation of sociomaterial assemblages enable people to think about potential for participation that they may not previously have seen as available to them. The critical question for participatory projects, then, is whether the sociomaterial configurations they make sensible create situations in which voices of dissensus can be heard. Design that makes it possible to hear dissensual voices creates opportunities for the dialogic of differently placed experts that can bring about change. As we discussed in chapter 4, this is Jeremy Till's (2005) negotiation of hope.

The critical dialogue concerning designing participatory projects can be seen at play in the invitation to take part, in the voices that take part, and in the texture of the dialogical spaces they create.

The Invitation to Take Part

The invitation to take part is the first point at which the particular distribution of the sensible and the mode of distributing the sensible intended for a project become apparent. As we will see in the following, the invitation can take a number of different forms, each of which aligns with pragmatic and critical aspects of participatory projects.

Taken first on a broad political scale, in a number of domains the invitation to participate has been criticized for neutralizing rather than empowering participants. Dave Beech, whose work we discussed in chapter 4, argues that for politics and art, participation has to do more than simply being seen to include those who are usually underrepresented. He argues that participation as inclusion or broadening engagement fails to realize the full potential of participation and can result in little more than tokenism. Worse still, he argues, that such logics and rhetoric tend to "neutralize" individuals by enculturating them in the unstated logic of someone else's invitation. What he has in mind here is the way in which participatory discourse around public activities and institutions can be used to neutralize dissensus, criticism, and the potential for conflict by presenting itself as a viable alternative to more radical change. In this context, the invitation to participate can be little more than a token gesture to deflect and appease.

Researchers approach participation in design enquiry with an aim in mind, and so, in a critical analysis, we have to wonder what researchers want from participants and vice versa. Participatory projects generally start with an invitation to participate, which can come from either researchers or participants. In participatory action research, for example, the invitation is often from a group in the community (e.g., community center, school, voluntary organization) who need some topic researched. In most of the projects we have discussed, the invitation originated with a researcher or research group who was seeking to explore a particular topic that other members of the public may be interested in or have more experience of. Wherever the invitation originates, it begins a process by which participants' subjectivities are framed and action potentials imagined. When it comes from the researchers, it can play a key role in forming the subjectivity of participants. It begins to tell them what sense of themselves as participants they may be expected to have, what position they are expected to take, and how much input they are likely to have in shaping the project and their own role in it. It can signal, for example, whether the project is intended to be a shared process of creative enquiry or an enquiry devised by the researcher for which input of some sort from participants is required.

The degree to which the terms of participation are preconfigured within the invitation or are allowed to evolve as the project proceeds indicates to participants the extent to which, and the ways in which, they may expect to be involved in shaping the roles that they will play. This should not be read as a simple relationship. As we have seen from Asher (Peltomäki

2010) and Deller's (2002, 2012) work, even when the terms of participation are largely preconfigured, an egalitarian and creative participation can still result. In some of their projects, participants can explore their own life stories and identities even within constraints set by the artist to ensure involvement of some institution. In their projects and in others, the tools and methods used can enable processes of self-configuration or scaffold preconfigured roles and values, and support, inhibit, or channel participants' experiences and expertise. Whether this process of configuration is done explicitly and made visible to participants or whether it is done more implicitly as framings and assumed pretexts raises critical questions for the design of participatory projects.

How an invitation frames the expected participation can also have a direct bearing on people's commitment to a project. For example, a direct invitation to participate in a project with the terms of participation included—as might happen when a project recruits participants by circulating an e-mail with project information and an indication of the commitment involved—is quite different from an invitation that follows from a period of volunteering and meeting with a group of people who are then invited to take part in the project. The latter, based on relationships that are already developing, can involve a more personal conversation constructed on some shared understanding and commitments.

Offering an invitation already presupposes a decision about who gets to participate. Within participatory design (PD), there is often a concern to involve those whose jobs and lives will be affected by the technology being designed. But not all those affected can possibly be included in the traditional PD workshop. Rather, the idea is that in some sense those who do take part will represent or stand proxy for this larger public. This logic of invitation frames the subjectivity of the participants as making the common knowledge or the common expertise of the public available to the design team. An alternative logic of this form of invitation is that by participating, these proxies have the design vision made available to them and come away as converts to technical imaginary and take the word back home to the public. A dialogical version of these logics is that both can operate simultaneously within an open creative space and what emerges as a design is recognizably owned by both parties.

Another logic of invitation is the demographic sampling approach in which representative samples of the public are preselected and invited. This logic was used by "Listening to the City," described in chapter 6, which is also an example of a highly preconfigured process in which not only roles, activities, and decision processes were carefully designed and managed but also the design space itself was preconfigured with possible solutions. Interesting then that the result of the process was to overturn that preconfigured space. Such a logic is a strong defense against the accusation of tokenism that can so easily be leveled at smaller-scale participatory projects of the sort typically seen in HCI and detailed in this book.

The participatory projects we have described in this book involve only between one and twenty or so members of the public. So what is the logic of participation in these cases? The first thing to note is that for many of these projects, participants are not configured as representative of, or as proxies for, other members of the public in the way we outlined previously. Neither are the projects configured as an open invitation to the public, as is the case in, for example, social media. In such cases, because people self-select, they are assumed to be the people who are most interested in the outcomes, and conversely those who self-select out are assumed to be disinterested in the outcomes. By contrast, for many the projects in this book, the invitation to participate is extended only to those who will be affected by whatever is designed. Importantly, unlike many PD projects, what will be designed or indeed whether anything will be designed has not been determined before the invitation to participate has been issued and accepted. In the Personhood, the Women's Centre, and the Spheres projects for example, the invitation to participate was precisely to those who would be the recipients of whatever was designed. In these cases, the hope was that those who took part in the design would find something meaningful (and hopefully memorable or even life-changing) in what was produced, which would be enough of an outcome for the design team and the participants.

By contrast, in projects like BOSOP, the aspiration was to find solutions that would help not just those who participated but also others in similar situations. The challenge of how to scale up or generalize can be addressed in many ways. First, a very simple response is to assume that although whatever has been produced has been produced in response to specific experiences of particular people or communities, nevertheless, because all artifacts are open to both interpretation and appropriation as they move through communities, others will find value and meaning in the artifact when it is put into circulation. This is the logic of inclusive design. Second, it may not be the designed artifact but the method of its production that is generalizable to other situations. This is a common response in HCI, with a range of methods for participatory design being put forward within academic journals and conferences and positioned in terms of the kinds of information or responses that each method is good for, inviting readers and audiences to imagine how the method might be suitably appropriated into a situation of interest to them. Third, the project as a whole can stand as a case study or a project-level demonstrator of what can be achieved in terms of a more holistic outcome, which includes not only the artifacts but also the collective experiences and shared understandings that have been gained by all of the participants. Here, as in participatory action research, the emphasis is much more on the mechanics of processes and the complexities of multistakeholder outcomes, and the kind of lessons learned that offer insights for other researchers with similar challenges. These lasting changes in social relationships, knowledge, and experience are often hard to articulate, but for those who have taken part, these are often the most significant outcomes.

Voices

Every person's voice is unique, and so too (to varying degrees) is their face, their body, their name, and crucially for our discussions, their biography, their history, and their experience. All of these aspects of individuals make them unique, and it is in this extended sense that we use the term *voice*. Voice is what makes a person unique and is also why he or she is invited to participate in a project.

As we have discussed elsewhere (Vines et al. 2013), up to a few years ago, participation in HCI meant involving users in design, following the user-centered or PD design traditions in which putative users of systems cooperate with designers in defining problems, identifying solutions, and evaluating designs. For the most part, PD involves getting people on board with a predefined project or helping people to define what they want or need in a predefined context. Simonsen and Robertson (2012, 27–28) identify the two fundamental aspects of PD as giving those people who are likely to use the technology a voice in its design and ensuring a process of mutual learning between designers and users to inform understanding of what future technologies and associated practices are likely to be.

In PD, the idea of *giving participants a voice* is often realized through their interactions with visualizations, prototypes, mockups, and other tools, and through their participation in staged design workshops. These are often seen as ways of drawing participants into working relationships with professional designers, in which participants are facilitated to imagine what new technology might bring and what they might want from it. The risk with structured approaches such as these is that the lived experience that participants bring to the project, and which is the reason for their participation, becomes reified through such abstractions, and its richness may be lost or reduced to evidence for or against a design proposition. Consequently, in many of the participatory projects in this book, the aim was to keep experience alive throughout the design process. In those projects, the ideas of giving users a voice and of democratizing designer-user relationships are extended. At the heart of this extended notion of participation is the difference between being *given a voice* and *having a voice*.

When *given a voice,* a speaker may feel limited by any social contract implied in the invitation to participate, for example, a contract that invites contributions about the quality of a prototype or the information needed in a specific setting. When *an already-existing voice is recognized,* that is when one's right to participate as oneself is realized and the value of dissensus is acknowledged, the assumption that the other already has a voice is recognition from the outset of the ethical and aesthetic value of the other's perspective. In the Jacob House and the Women's Centre projects, the researchers responded to caution, resistance, and antagonism by finding ways to bring the already active voices of the participants to the fore, avoiding the kind of crude or tokenistic participation that draws people into activities over which they feel no ownership.

In participatory projects such as these, the assumption is that researchers and participants will have something to learn from each other. A more typical professional relationship involves clients moving from the space of their own experience and expertise toward the educated, expert position (and voice) of the professional in a bid to "keep up" and in the hope of better seeing and making sense of their own experience. By contrast, in the approach taken in the Women's Centre and Jacob House projects, ways are found for all dissenting voices to find a potential space "inbetween" self and other. This approach resonates with Cruikshank's analysis of the localized knowledge and social imagination that emerges from encounters with strangers working creatively with each other.

Many of the projects we have considered involve a deeply situated engagement with people in their own life worlds, whether that is while having fun at an open-air spectacle or working out how to live with dementia. Going into those places in which participants live and make sense of their own experience involves encountering people where they already have a voice. These are also settings in which recognition of the voices of researchers and designers cannot be assumed. In such settings, researchers and designers have to spend time establishing their credentials, explaining what they are about, and making clear that they understand that they are operating in the other's place, a place where they are outsiders and have to find or even create roles for themselves. In these cases, researchers have to learn about the ways in which they may be allowed to participate, not just about how other participants might want to participate.

Voice then, in the extended sense we have developed in this analysis, can be understood only relationally. A voice is not a voice if it is not heard and responded to by another, and who "the other" is depends critically on where the encounter takes place. This relationality drives to the heart of many of the difficulties and tensions experienced in participatory projects, whether standing up in front of an audience and improvising with musicians or standing up as a health worker in a room full of patients to explain the "book of bullshit."

The Texture of Dialogical Spaces

A dialogic approach can sometimes come across as simply drawing attention to the potential of communication between people, generally between two people. Carefully listening to the other in order to be responsive to their experience suggests movement toward resolution. But as we have seen throughout this book, the interconnections between researchers and participants, situations and things, and how they are experienced individually and collectively in participatory projects is more complex and nuanced than this. The tensions between belonging and identity, privacy and disclosure, trust and vulnerability are made sensible through the complex mesh of interconnections among researchers, participants, and situations. It is in dealing with this complexity that a dialogical approach gains traction. A dialogical approach is open to the possibility that there is no resolution, that experience and meanings remain unfinalized and plural. It is a process of engagement that makes sensible difference and dissensus beyond the focal communication and that brings history into the present and projects into the future, creating a complex texture of interconnections across time and space, between people and things.

Texture is often thought of as the perceived surface quality of a work, which in art and design can be used to convey information about function or style and emotional quality. As we have seen, surface matters in participatory projects as the space in which people find ways of belonging and interacting together. The texture of dialogical space describes the ways in which networks of affect and value are positioned in language and other embodied interaction. It is not a texture of language or sounds; rather, it is a texture of one-off meaningful moments in which acts inflected by emotion and volition carve out the boundaries and thresholds that make participative experience sensible to those involved.

We have variously referred to boundaries and thresholds when discussing the spaces in which participants encounter each other. For example, in chapter 6, Hauser's "permeable boundaries" helped us to describe people's engagement with each other in media publics. Although *boundary* is probably the more widely used term in HCI, threshold has something different to offer in terms of understanding the communities of sense that characterize participatory projects. Its evocation of entrances, passages, and doorways suggests an experience that is beginning or about to begin and evokes people not just moving across but also looking into and looking out onto. The ambiguity of where a threshold begins or ends is redolent of the kind of "inbetween" belonging we have used to understand some participatory experiences. It also resonates with Rancière's sensible, because it refers to the level at which sensations can be detected. Thresholds evoke beginnings and openings in contrast with the limits suggested by boundaries. It provides opportunities for looking across without crossing or for preparing for a change in the texture of dialogical space before crossing.

We think of communities of sense as self-organizing and internally regulating, generating their own thresholds through controlling what is made sensible within their community. But they also have half an eye on what is going on outside, across the threshold of the community, and how they present themselves to the outside. Probyn's outside belonging on balconies in Montreal describes a rhythmic movement between private and public played out across thresholds that subtly manage availability. The texture of participation and belonging can be more layered in many participatory projects when, for example, researchers developing close relationships with participants must also keep an eye on personal and ethical aspects of sharing the experience with other communities when publishing their research. For example, in the Women's Centre project described in chapter 5, domestic violence, voice, disclosure, and vulnerability are intimately linked as the researcher and women explore modes of self-expression that enable sharing within while preserving anonymity without.

Communities of sense can be defined by sets of manners of being and responding to what is sensible and what is not sensible. The associated ways of acting and making sense of what happens may be sensible only to those inside and may not make sense at all outside. In the BOSOP project described in chapter 4, the process of participation was deliberately engineered to make thresholds visible and to enable each group to determine issues of disclosure across them. As mentioned previously, within one community (the nursing staff), the "book of bullshit" was made sensible in an early meeting. But with an eye to the inevitable threshold crossing that the design process entailed, its original title was covered over by a sticky note reading "standard excuses" before presentation at the joint meeting. But at that joint meeting, a member of staff peeled off the "standard excuses" to reveal the original "book of bullshit" title and referred to it as such in her presentation. This is an example of a one-off meaningful moment in which the particular intonation of an act defines a threshold that needed to be passed through in order that the group could move on. The same gesture in another context may have had no effect at all. A community of sense then is a contoured and changing space of relationships and relevance, sense is contingently carved out of the dissensus of voices and values, the manners conjugated enabling collaboration among people with very different backgrounds and interests.

In the networked publics that we discussed in chapter 6, we can clearly see participant subjectivity emerge as people position themselves as players in social media interaction. As they do so, they create the thresholds and manners of being that define the scope of their participation. We saw the consequences of permeability in chapter 6, when Pete was tagged by one of his daughters in a photo of him she posted for fun. As social media participants become more aware of these consequences, they learn to ameliorate them by using the resources available in the medium to configure their participation as they would like it. One of John's students carried out a study of students' strategic impression management on Facebook in which she found participants developing a variety of tactics to manage their exposure (Feehan, in press). Many had two sites, one of which is very open but not easily traceable to them and the other of which is tailored to show them in a good light, for example, to prospective employers.

This suggests that the key thing for participants is the *community of sense*, the "contingent and non-essential manner of being together in community" (Hinderliter et al. 2009, 2) that the participants take part in. It can be defined by the invitation to take part in a relatively closed participatory project or it can be as open as participants configuring their own involvement in their own social media spaces. Or it can be layered, as BOSOP was, with staff and patients meeting the project teams separately first and then gradually moving across traditional and professional boundaries.

Thinking about the invitation to participate, voice and dissensus, and the texture of dialogical space has provided us with a critical space to learn how participatory projects reconfigure participation and enrich participative experience. We now go on to consider the second way in which we have learned from engaging with these projects, about epistemology and enquiry in HCI and design, and, in particular, the potential that participatory projects offer for HCI to move beyond user-centered and participatory design.

Design Enquiry as Critical Dialogue

Our particular contribution to understanding the nature of participative experience has been in bringing together a dialogical approach to participation and a critical questioning of what is made sensible in participatory projects. This has supported the critical dialogue that has been developed through chapters 3 to 6 around the nature and value of participative experience as it relates to participatory design projects more generally. The purpose is not to police what counts as participatory or to reinforce a particular definition of quality in participatory projects. Rather the purpose is to clarify what we can learn from these participatory projects about the potential for HCI to move beyond user-centered and participatory design as traditionally conceived in HCI. Specifically, we have learned from the values embodied in these projects about the changing nature of relationships in HCI projects, the technological imaginaries they seek to nurture, and the subjective positionings they seek to configure in their projects. To us, these all seem to be redolent of a new egalitarian sensibility in design.

The critical dialogue we have in mind is different from that typically employed in social theory. Critical thinking in social theory is generally understood as involving a suspicious stance toward interpretation based on the idea that there is always something hidden behind the appearance of the social. Adopting such a critical stance would put us in a position with respect to the participatory HCI projects that we have avoided from the outset, a position of claiming to know better and to see what is behind those projects. It would also be at odds with the emphasis on local knowledge and imagination that we have appropriated from Cruikshank's work in chapter 3. The critical dialogue we have engendered acknowledges that "there is no hidden secret of the machine ... no lost unity to reappropriate" (Rancière 2009b, 32). Instead it is marked by a strong sense of learning from and with the projects and the experiences of the researchers and participants involved in them. Rancière's analysis of dissensus offers a way in which such a critical dialogue can be opened up. Starting a critical dialogue from a position that values dissensus removes the fundamental distrust of experience that a search for unity provokes and starts instead from an appreciation of the variety of ways that people have of making sense of experience.

For Rancière consensus is commitment to a belief in a world in which everything has its proper place and function "without remainder," a world in which there are no outsiders just dropouts. Dissensus is a form of innovation, which is not outside of consensus but is enabled by it, which challenges the current hierarchy and the policing of domains within the consensus. Dissensus is not a destructive impulse borne out of conflict and suspicion; it is a creative act, "a division inserted in 'common sense'" (Rancière 2010, 69), which seeks to question what is commonly accepted without thought or question. Although consensus is defined by a distribution of the sensible that makes its rules commonsense and thus unquestionable, dissensus is characterized by an "an innovative leap from the logic that ordinarily governs human situations" (Corcoran 2010, 1). This innovative leap requires an ability first to imagine and then to articulate an alternative logic or a different way of looking that offers a meaningful way of going on. Politics and art for Rancière are examples of dissensual practices and

the disruption that they [politics and art] effect is not simply a reordering of the relations of power between existing groups; dissensus is not an institutional overturning. It is an activity that cuts across forms of cultural and identity belonging and hierarchies between discourses and genres, working to introduce new subjects and heterogeneous objects into the field of perception. (Corcoran 2010, 2)

With respect to HCI, the kinds of participatory projects we have considered in this book raise voices of dissent that open up critical dialogue around questions such as, who initiates and benefits from participation in design? Who gets to participate, how do they get to participate, and why? How is control shared and why (Vines et al. 2013)? They raise questions about how researchers and participants are and could be configured, what it means for a project to be ethical, and how the outcomes of such projects should be judged. For me (Pete), a personally insightful moment occurred during the BOSOP project when the following question struck me: if our patients are here as equal but differently placed experts, why aren't they being paid for their work in the same way the design team are? By raising such critical questions participatory projects contribute to critical dialogues about what HCI could be.

HCI as a discipline has always thrived on dissensus. In its earliest conception, psychologists came together with computer scientists to challenge unquestioned assumptions about how to design and develop technology and to make sensible constructs such as "the user" and "usability" as "new subjects and new heterogeneous objects" (Corcoran 2010, 2). Later work sought to challenge unquestioned assumptions about distinctions such as designers, users, and technology. For quite a while now there has also been an impetus to explore new ways of doing research, new ways of constituting the interdisciplinary field, and new disciplines coming into dialogue. Learning with and from participants as well as from a variety of disciplines has been an engine of change within HCI as its digital imaginary has evolved. The idea of HCI as an interdiscipline captures something of the way in which it dwells in between other disciplines in order to have a fluid and responsive practice. Its community exists in a kind of outside belonging, neither computer science nor psychology, engineering nor design, art nor science. Outside belonging is a dissensual existence and it is one of HCI's major strengths when dealing with the social contexts out of which thinking and feeling emerge and when designing on the threshold between the individual and the collective.

In Conclusion

For us, researching this book has been a process of discovery. It started with our enchantment with Haque's participatory events. It ends with a sense of fellow-travel with Tim Ingold in his latest book.

In his book *Making*, anthropologist Tim Ingold (2013, 2) described anthropology as the most "anti-academic of academic disciplines." Rancière would recognize dissensus in Ingold's account of anthropology. Although sustained by the institutions of higher education, Ingold argues that anthropology is dedicated to challenging the epistemological claims on which those same institutions are built and that underwrite their operations. The claims in question are the claims of the institution to holding the authoritative account on the reality behind appearances.

In the academic pantheon, reason is predestined to trump intuition, expertise to trump commonsense, and conclusions based on the facts to trump what people know from ordinary experience or from the wisdom of forebears. (Ingold 2013, 2)

Ingold would agree with Rancière that "there is no hidden secret of the machine" (Rancière 2009b, 32). For Ingold, anthropology turns the epistemology of the institution on its head by starting from the assumption that if anyone knows anything of the ways of the world it will be those who have dedicated their lives to following them.

Cruikshank's local knowledge, Rancière's dissensus, the critical concepts of dialogue, "inbetweeness," and participation all come together in this egalitarian sensibility, and participatory projects in HCI share this commitment to an epistemology that challenges and transforms the concept of research and academic enquiry. A transformation that is echoed in movements such as the Civic University, located in and responsive to the cities they inhabit (Goddard and Vallance 2013), citizen science, crowdsourcing, digital civics, and participatory cultures.

Ingold also distinguished between anthropology and ethnography. For Ingold, ethnography is concerned with the study and documentation of the lives and times of the community that hosts the researcher. In so doing its impulse is to look back to account for how things are. By contrast, anthropology is concerned to study *with* people and to learn *from* them and to use what they learn to move forward. Whereas ethnography is documentary, he argues, anthropology is transformational. Ingold argues that anthropologist and ethnographer are often combined within a single researcher, and the tasks can proceed in tandem. The point is, however, that they are not the same way of looking, and they require different subjective positionings in relation to the enquiry.

If we were to draw a parallel between Ingold's analysis and our understanding of the design enquiries we have discussed in this book, it would be that participatory design projects in HCI, similar to Ingold's anthropology, seek to learn *with* and *from* those who take part in design enquiry, and they do so in order to move forward. HCI and design in general tends to be resistant to easy definitions, and participatory projects even more so. But whatever else is true, HCI is a forward looking and dissensual discipline that seeks to create technological imaginaries with people, through which we can move forward in a way that is true to an epistemology of experience.

Appendix: Web Resources and Videos of Projects

This is a collection of web resources and videos that we found to be a useful visual complement to the published academic papers about the projects that we describe in this book. We hope you may find them useful, too.

The Battle of Orgreave

http://www.artangel.org.uk/projects/2001/the_battle_of_orgreave
http://www.youtube.com/watch?v=3ncrWxnxLjg

Bespoke

http://www.dwrc.surrey.ac.uk/bespoke.shtml

Blacksburg Electronic Village

http://www.bev.net

BOSOP

http://www.uchd.org.uk/uchd-in-action/outpatient-services

DiabetesMine

http://www.diabetesmine.com/about

dream.Medusa

http://webdocs.cs.ualberta.ca/~robyn/dreamMedusa2.mov

https://www.youtube.com/watch?v=lDYjlfgEQNQ

FolkArchive

http://www.britishcouncil.org/folkarchive/folk.html

GalaxyZoo

http://www.galaxyzoo.org

Humanaquarium

http://www.robyntaylor.com/humanaquarium.html
http://www.youtube.com/watch?v=zTrWjSp1cF4
http://www.youtube.com/watch?v=C0uWEzweV44
http://www.wired.co.uk/news/archive/2010-03/16/humanaquarium
-two-musicians-one-large-box

Jacob House

http://markblythe.me.uk/MarkBlythe/The_Photostroller.html

Joy in People

http://www.youtube.com/watch?v=8Wl8OYZB6As
http://www.youtube.com/watch?v=HKZz-AeEWqU

Listening to the City

http://americaspeaks.org/projects/topics/disaster-recovery/listening
-to-the-city

Mobility and Place Project (MyPLACE)

http://gow.epsrc.ac.uk/NGBOViewGrant.aspx?GrantRef=EP/K037366/1

Open Burble

http://www.haque.co.uk/openburble.php

http://www.youtube.com/watch?v=g0w7i-xkQNs
http://www.haque.co.uk/burblelondon.php

Personhood

http://www.northumbria.ac.uk/sd/academic/scd/research/casestudies/
jaynewallaceproject
http://www.youtube.com/watch?v=RFrs-0rW6g8
http://vimeo.com/19431560

The Photostroller

http://www.gold.ac.uk/media/Photostroller.pdf
http://markblythe.me.uk/MarkBlythe/The_Photostroller.html

Prayer Companion

http://markblythe.me.uk/MarkBlythe/Prayer_Companion/Prayer_
Companion.html
https://www.moma.org/interactives/exhibitions/2011/talktome/objects
/145526

Sky Ear

http://www.haque.co.uk/skyear
http://vimeo.com/1531759
http://www.rmg.co.uk/explore/art/new-visions/usman-haque-sky-ear
http://www.soundtoys.net/toys/sky-ear
http://www.youtube.com/watch?v=ln-zJwxjOJ0

Social Inclusion through the Digital Economy Research Hub (SiDE)

http://www.side.ac.uk

The Spheres of Wellbeing

http://di.ncl.ac.uk/phd-projects/thieme
http://homepages.cs.ncl.ac.uk/anja.thieme/spheres.html

Storybank

http://www.dwrc.surrey.ac.uk/storybank.shtml
http://www.tellingstorybank.info

Urban Remix

http://urbanremix.gatech.edu

VJs

http://homepages.cs.ncl.ac.uk/jonathan.hook/documentaryvj.php
http://www.youtube.com/watch?v=f0iFs1KvBTA

The Women's Centre

http://di.ncl.ac.uk/phd-projects/clarke/

The Wray Village, RuralConnect LivingLab

http://www.infolab21.co.uk/livinglab

References

Adams, T. 2012. Galaxy Zoo and the New Dawn of Citizen Science. *The Guardian*, March 17. Available at http://www.guardian.co.uk/science/2012/mar/18/galaxy-zoo -crowdsourcing-citizen-scientists.

Agamben, G. 1993. *The Coming Community*. University of Minnesota Press.

Ahmed, S. 2004. *The Cultural Politics of Emotion*. Routledge.

Anderson, R., L. A. Baxter, and K. N. Cissna, eds. 2004. *Dialogue: Theorizing Difference in Communication Studies*. Sage.

Arendt, H. 1958. *The Human Condition*. University of Chicago Press.

Arnstein, S. R. 1969. A Ladder of Citizen Participation. *Journal of the American Institute of Planners* 35 (4):216–224.

Bakhtin, M. 1984. *Problems of Dostoevsky's Poetics*. University of Minnesota Press.

Bakhtin, M. 1986. *Speech Genres and Other Late Essays*. University of Texas Press.

Bate, P., and G. Robert. 2007. *Bringing User Experience to Healthcare Improvement: The Concepts, Methods and Practices of Experience-Based Design*. Radcliffe Publishing.

Bauman, Z. 2001. *Community: Seeking Safety in an Insecure World*. Polity Press.

BBC. 2011. Strictly Come Dancing Blog. Available at http://www.bbc.co.uk/blogs/ strictlycomedancing/2011/10/week-3---leaderboard.shtml#more.

BBC. 2014. Orgreave Campaigners Call for BBC Strike Coverage Apology. Available at: http://www.bbc.co.uk/news/uk-england-south-yorkshire-27893072.

Beech, D. 2008. Include Me Out! *Art Monthly* 8 (4):1–4.

Belenky, M. F., B. M. Clinchy, N. R. Goldberger, and J. M. Tarule. 1997. *Women's Ways of Knowing: The Development of Self, Voice and Mind. Tenth Anniversary Edition*. Basic Books.

Benford, S., A. Crabtree, S. Reeves, J. Sheridan, A. Dix, M. Flintham, and A. Drozd. 2006. The Frame of the Game: Blurring the Boundary between Fiction and Reality in

Mobile Experiences. In *Proceedings of ACM CHI 2006 Conference on Human Factors in Computing Systems*, 427–436. ACM Press.

Benhabib, S. 1992. *Situating the Self: Gender, Community and Postmodern Contemporary Ethics*. Polity Press.Bishop, C. 2011. Zones of Indistinguishability: Collective Actions Group and Participatory Art. *e-flux journal* 29 (November).

Bishop, C. 2012. *Artificial Hells: Participatory Art and the Politics of Spectatorship*. Verso.

Blythe, M., P. Wright, J. Bowers, A. Boucher, N. Jarvis, P. Reynolds, and B. Gaver. 2010. Age and Experience: Ludic Engagement in a Residential Care Setting. *Proceedings of DIS* 10:161–170.

Blum-Ross, A., J. Mills, P. Egglestone, and D. M. Frohlich. 2013. Community Media and Design: Insight Journalism As a Method for Innovation. *Journal of Media Practice* 14 (3):171–192.

Bødker, S. 2006. When Second-Wave HCI Meets Third-Wave Challenges. *Proceedings of NordiCHI* 06:1–8.

Bowen, S., D. Dearden, D. Wolstenholme, and M. Cobb. 2011. Different Views: Including Others in Participatory Health Service Innovation. In *Proceedings of the Second Participatory Innovation Conference*, 230–236. University of Southern Denmark.

Bowman, P., and R. Stamp, eds. 2011. *Reading Rancière*. Continuum.

Brown, J. S., and P. Duguid. 1996. Keeping It Simple. In *Bringing Design to Software*, ed. T. Winograd, 129–145. Addison Wesley.

Burke, K. 1973. *The Philosophy of Literary Form*. 3rd ed. University of California Press.

Carroll, J. M., and M. B. Rosson. 1996. Developing the Blacksburg Electronic Village. *Communications of the ACM* 30 (12):69–74.

Carroll, J. M., and M. B. Rosson. 2007. Participatory Design in Community Informatics. *Design Studies* 28:243–261.

Civic Alliance to Rebuild Downtown New York. 2002. *Listening to the City: Report of Proceedings*. Available at http://americaspeaks.org/wp-content/_data/n_0001/resources /live/final_report_ltc3.pdf.

Clarke, R., P. Wright, M. Balaam, and J. McCarthy. 2013 Digital Portraits: Photosharing after Domestic Violence. *Proceedings of ACM CHI 2013 Conference on Human Factors in Computing Systems*, 429–438. ACM Press.

Cleaver, F. 2001. Institutions, Agency and the Limitations of Participatory Approaches to Development. In *Participation: The New Tyranny?*, ed. B. Cook and U. Kothari, 36–55. Zed Books.

Conley, T. M. 1979. Ancient Rhetoric and Modern Genre Criticism. *Communication Quarterly* 27 (4):47–53.

Cook, B., and U. Kothari. 2001. *Participation: The New Tyranny?* Zed Books.

Corcoran, S. 2010. Editor's Introduction. In J. Rancière, *Dissensus: On Politics and Aesthetics*, 1–24. Bloomsbury.

Cottam, H., and C. Leadbetter. 2004. *Health: Co-creating Services.* RED Paper 01. London: Design Council.

Cruikshank, J. 2005. *Do Glaciers Listen? Local Knowledge, Colonial Encounters and Social Imagination.* University of British Columbia Press.

Dasgupta, S. 2008. Art Is Going Nowhere and Politics Has to Catch It: An Interview with Jacques Rancière. *Krisis* 1:70–76.

Deetz, S., and J. Simpson. 2004. Critical Organizational Dialogue: Open Formation and the Demand of "Otherness." In *Dialogue: Theorizing Difference in Communication Studies*, ed. R. Anderson, L. A. Baxter, and K. N. Cissna, 141–158. Sage.

Deller, J. 2002. *The English Civil War: Part II: Personal Accounts of the 1984–85 Miners' Strike.* Artangel.

Deller, J. 2012. *Joy in People.* Hayward Publishing.

Dewey, J. 1925. *Experience and Nature.* Open Court Publishing.

Dewey, J. 1927. *The Public and Its Problems.* Holt.

Diocaretz, M. 2006. Interactivity and the Information Society Technological Imaginary. *Acta Poetica* 27 (1):115–139.

DiSalvo, C. 2012. *Adversarial Design.* MIT Press.

Eco, U. 1989. *The Open Work.* Harvard University Press.

Feehan, C. In press. "… There Is a Kind of Way of Being on Facebook": A Thematic Analysis of the Production of Self-presentation on the Social Networking site Facebook. *Psychology & Society.*

Forester, J. 1985. Designing: Making Sense Together in Practical Conversations. *Journal of Architectural Education* 38 (3):14–20.

Foucault, M. 1984. Sex, Power, and the Politics of Identity. In *Foucault Live: Collected Interviews, 1961–1984*, ed. Sylvère Lotringer. Semiotext(e).

Frohlich, D. M., and D. Rachovides, R. Kriaki, R. Bhat, M. Frank, E. Erdirisinghe, W. Dhammike, M. Jones, and W. Harwood. 2009. StoryBank: Mobile Digital Storytelling in a Development Context. In *Proceedings of ACM CHI 2009 Conference on Human Factors in Computing Systems*, 1761–1770. ACM Press.

Frohlich, D. M., K. Smith, A. Blum-Ross, P. Egglestone, J. Mills, S. Smith, J. Rogers, M. Shorter, J. Marshall, P. Olivier, J. Woods, J. Wallace, G. Wood, and M. Blythe. 2011. Crossing the Digital Divide in the Other Direction: Community-centred Design on the Bespoke Project. *Proceedings of Include 2011*, Royal College of Art, London. Available at http://include11.kinetixevents.co.uk/rca/rca2011/paper_final/F387_2269.PDF.

Gaver, B., M. Blythe, A. Boucher, N. Jarvis, J. Bowers, and P. Wright. 2010. The Prayer Companion: Openness and Specificity, Materiality and Spirituality. In *Proceedings of ACM CHI 2010 Conference on Human Factors in Computing Systems*, 2055–2064. ACM Press.

Gaver, B., P. Wright, A. Boucher, J. Bowers, M. Blythe, N. Jarvis, D. Cameron, T. Kerridge, A. Wilkie, and R. Phillips. 2011. The Photostroller: Supporting Diverse Care Home Residents in Engaging with the World. *Proceedings of ACM CHI 2011 Conference on Human Factors in Computing Systems*, 1757–1766. ACM Press.

Giaccardi. E. 2012. *Heritage and Social Media*. Routledge.

Ginwright, S., P. Noguera, and J. Cammarota. 2006. *Beyond Resistance! Youth Activism and Community Change*. Routledge.

Goddard, J., and P. Vallance. 2013. *The University and the City*. Routledge.

Gormley, A. 2008. Antony Gormley Interviewed by Hans Ulrich Obrist. Catalogue. Museo de Arte Contemporaneo, Monterrey, Mexico. Available at www.antonygormley.com/resources/download-text/id/117.

Guardian. 2012. Miners' Strike: Police to Be Investigated over "Battle of Orgreave." Available at http://www.theguardian.com/uk/2012/nov/16/miners-strike-police-battle-orgreave.

Hall, S. 2012. Jeremy Deller's Political Imaginary. In J. Deller, *Joy in People*, 81–90. Hayward Publishing.

Haque, U. 2010. Invited Design Speaker. SIGCHI Conference on Human Factors in Computing CHI 2010. Available at http://dl.acm.org/citation.cfm?id=1753326.2167164&coll=DL&dl=GUIDE&CFID=364750897&CFTOKEN=53526987.

Hauser, G. A. 1999. *Vernacular Voices: The Rhetoric of Publics and Public Spheres*. University of South Carolina Press.

Hinderliter, B., W. Kaizen, V. Maimon, J. Mansoor, and S. McCormick, eds. 2009. *Communities of Sense: Rethinking Aesthetics and Politics*. Duke University Press.

Hodges, D. 1998. Participation as Dis-identification with/in a Community of Practice. *Mind, Culture, and Activity* 5 (4):272–290.

Hook, J., D. Green, J. McCarthy, S. Taylor, P. Wright, and P. Olivier. 2011. A VJ-Centered Exploration of Expressive Interaction. In *Proceedings of ACM CHI 2011 Conference on Human Factors in Computing Systems*, 1265–1274. ACM Press.

Hook, J., J. McCarthy, P. Wright, and P. Olivier. 2013. Waves: Exploring Idiographic Design for Live Performance. In *Proceedings of ACM CHI 2013 Conference on Human Factors in Computing Systems*, 2969–2978. ACM Press.

HoSang. D. 2006. Beyond Policy: Ideology, Race, and the Reimagining of Youth. In *Beyond Resistance! Youth Activism and Community Change*, ed. S. Ginwright, P. Noguera, and J. Cammarota, 3–20. Routledge.

Ingold, T. 2013. *Making*. Routledge.

Jackson, D., J. Nicholson, G. Stoeckigt, R. Wrobel, A. Thieme, and P. Olivier. 2013. Panopticon: A Parallel Video Overview System. *Proceedings of UIST* 13:123–130.

Jenkins, H. 2006. *Convergence Culture: Where Old and New Media Collide*. New York University Press.

Jenkins, H., R. Purushotma, M. Weigel, K. Clinton, and A. J. Robison. 2009. *Confronting the Challenges of Participatory Culture: Media Education for the Twenty-first Century*. MIT Press.

Kaprow, A. 2003. *Essays on the Blurring of Art and Life*. Ed. J. Kelley. University of California Press.

Kester, G. 2004. *Conversation Pieces: Community and Communication in Modern Art*. University of California Press.

Kuznetsov, S., A. S. Taylor, T. Regan, N. Villar, and E. Paulos. 2012. At the Seams: DIYbio and Opportunities for HCI. *Proceedings of DIS'12 Designing Interactive Systems Conference*, 258–267. ACM Press.

Lave, J., and E. Wenger. 1991. *Situated Learning: Legitimate Peripheral Participation*. Cambridge University Press.

Le Dantec, C. A. 2012. Participation and Publics: Supporting Community Engagement. In *Proceedings of ACM CHI 2012 Conference on Human Factors in Computing Systems*, 1351–1360. ACM Press.

Lim, M., and M. Kann. 2008. Politics: Deliberation, Mobilization and Networked Practices of Agitation. In *Networked Publics*, ed. K. Varnelis, 77–107. MIT Press.

Lindtner, S., J. Chen, G. Hayes, and P. Dourish. 2011. Towards a Framework of Publics: Re-encountering Media Sharing and Its User. *ACM Transactions on Human Computer Interaction* 18 (2):1–23.

McCarthy, J., and P. Wright. 2004. *Technology as Experience*. MIT Press.

Miller, C. R. 1984. Genre as Social Action. *Quarterly Journal of Speech* 70:151–167.

Miller, C. R. 1994. Rhetorical Community: The Cultural Basis of Genre. In *Genre and the New Rhetoric*, ed. A. Freedman and P. Medway, 67–78. Taylor and Francis.

Mosse, D. 2001. People's Knowledge, Participation and Patronage: Operations and Representations in Rural Development. In *Participation: The New Tyranny?*, ed. B. Cook and U. Kothari, 16–35. Zed Books.

Nancy, J.-L. 2001. *Being Singular Plural*. Stanford University Press.

Patton, J. H. 1976. Generic Criticism: Typology at an Inflated Price. *Rhetoric Social Quarterly* 6:4–8.

Peltomäki, K. 2010. *Situation Aesthetics: The Work of Michael Asher*. MIT Press.

Ploderer, B., P. Wright, S. Howard, and P. Thomas. 2009. "No Pain, No Gain": Pleasure and Suffering in Technologies of "Leidenschaft." *Interaction* 16 (5):6–11.

Probyn, E. 1996. *Outside Belongings*. Routledge.

Punt, M. 2000. *Early Cinema and the Technological Imaginary*. Postdigital Press. Thesis.

Rancière, J. 1991. *The Ignorant Schoolmaster: Five Lessons in Intellectual Emancipation*. Stanford University Press.

Rancière, J. 2006. *The Politics of Aesthetics: The Distribution of the Sensible*. Continuum International Publishing.

Rancière, J. 2009a. Contemporary Art and the Politics of Aesthetics. In *Communities of Sense: Rethinking Aesthetics and Politics*, ed. B. Hinderliter, W. Kaizen, V. Maimon, J. Mansoor, and S. McCormick, 31–50. Duke University Press.

Rancière, J. 2009b. *The Emancipated Spectator*. Verso.

Rancière, J. 2010. *Dissensus: On Politics and Aesthetics*. Bloomsbury.

Reason, P., and H. Bradbury, eds. 2001. *Handbook of Action Research: Participative Inquiry and Practice*. Sage.

Sanoff, H. 2000. *Community Participation Methods in Design and Planning*. Wiley.

Sacks, H. 1992. *Lectures on Conversation*. Vols. 1–2. Blackwell.

Sengers, P., and B. Gaver. 2006. Staying Open to Interpretation: Engaging Multiple Meanings in Design and Evaluation. *Proceedings of DIS*:99–108.

Shotter, J. 2000. Inside Dialogical Realities: From an Abstract-Systematic to a Participatory-Wholistic Understanding of Communication. *Southern Communication Journal* 65 (2):119–132.

Simon, N. 2010. *The Participatory Museum*. Museum 2.0.

Simonsen, J., and T. Robertson. 2012. *Routledge International Handbook of Participatory Design*. Routledge.

Studdert, D. 2006. *Conceptualising Community*. Palgrave MacMillan.

Suchman, L. 2007. *Human-Machine Reconfigurations: Plans and Situated Actions*. 2nd ed. Cambridge University Press.

Sullivan, P., and J. McCarthy. 2005. A Dialogical Approach to Experience-Based Inquiry. *Theory and Psychology* 15 (5):621–638.

Tanaka, A. 2006. Interaction, Agency, Experience, and the Future of Music. In *Consuming Music Together: Social and Collaborative Aspects of Music Consumption Technologies*, ed. B. Brown and K. O'Hara, 271–292. Springer.

Taylor, N., K. Cheverst, P. Wright, and P. Olivier. 2013. Leaving the Wild: Lessons from Community Technology Handovers. In *Proceedings of ACM CHI 2013 Conference on Human Factors in Computing Systems*, 1549–1558. ACM Press.

Taylor, N., J. Marshall, A. Blum-Ross, J. Mills, J. Rogers, P. Egglestone, D. M. Frohlich, P. Wright, and P. Olivier. 2012. Viewpoint: Empowering Communities with Situated Voting Devices. In *Proceedings of ACM CHI 2012 Conference on Human Factors in Computing Systems*, 1361–1370. ACM Press.

Taylor, R., P. Boulanger, and P. Olivier. 2008. dream.Medusa: A Participatory Performance. In *Proceedings of the Ninth International Symposium on Smart Graphics*, 200–206. Springer.

Taylor, R., G. Schofield, J. Shearer, J. Wallace, P. Wright, P. Boulanger, and P. Olivier. 2011b. Humanaquarium: Exploring Audience, Participation, and Interaction. In *Proceedings of ACM CHI 2011 Conference on Human Factors in Computing Systems*, 1855–1864. ACM Press.

Taylor, R., G. Schofield, J. Shearer, J. Wallace, P. Wright, P. Boulanger, and P. Olivier. 2011a. *Designing from Within: Humanaquarium*. In *Proceedings of ACM CHI 2011 Conference on Human Factors in Computing Systems*, 1117–1122. ACM Press.

Taylor, R. 2012. *Designing from Within: Exploring Experience through Interactive Performance*. PhD thesis, University of Alberta.

Thieme, A., J. Wallace, J. McCarthy, S. Lindley, P. Wright, P. Olivier, and T. D. Meyer. 2013. Design to Promote Mindfulness Practice and Sense of Self for Vulnerable Psychiatric Patients in Secure Services. In *Proceedings of the ACM CHI 2013 Conference on Human Factors in Computing Systems*, 2647–2656. ACM Press.

Till, J. 2005. The Negotiation of Nope. In *Architecture and Participation*, ed. P. Blundell Jones, D. Petrescu, and J. Till, 19–41. Spon Press Taylor Francis Group.

Turner, G. 1988. *Film as Social Practice*. Routledge.

Varnelis, K., ed. 2012. *Networked Publics*. MIT Press.

Verasawmy, R., and O. S. Iversen. 2012. Bannerbattle: Introducing Crowd Experience to Interaction Design. In *Proceedings of the Seventh Nordic Conference on Human-Computer Interaction*, 228–237. ACM Press.

Vines, J., R. Clarke, P. Wright, J. McCarthy, and P. Olivier. 2013. Configuring Participation: On How We Involve People in Design. In *Proceedings of ACM CHI 2013 Conference on Human Factors in Computing Systems*, 429–438. ACM Press.

Walkerdine, V. 2010. Communal Beingness and Affect: An Exploration of Trauma in an Ex-industrial Community. *Body & Society* 16 (1):91–116.

Wallace, J., P. Wright, J. McCarthy, D. Green, J. Thomas, and P. Olivier. 2013. A Design-Led Inquiry into Personhood in Dementia. In *Proceedings of ACM CHI 2013 Conference on Human Factors in Computing Systems*, 2617–2626. ACM Press.

Warner, M. 2002. *Publics and Counterpublics*. Zone Books.

Webster, C. 2002. *The National Health Service: A Political History*. 2nd ed. Oxford University Press.

Williams, R. 1977. *Marxism and Literature*. Oxford University Press.

Wittgenstein, L. 1953. *Philosophical Investigations*. Blackwell.

Wright, P. 2011. Reconsidering the H, the C, and the I: Some Thoughts on Reading Suchman's Human-Machine Reconfigurations in HCI. *Interaction* 18 (5):28–31.

Wright, P. C., and J. McCarthy. 2008. Experience and Empathy in HCI. In *Proceedings of ACM CHI 2008 Conference on Human Factors in Computing Systems*, 637–646. ACM Press.

Wright, P., and J. McCarthy. 2010. *Experience-Centered Design: Designers, Users, and Communities in Dialogue*. Morgan Claypool.

Index

Printed in the United States
by Baker & Taylor Publisher Services